# The Joiner/Ryals Family

Maxine Ellis Griner

HERITAGE BOOKS
2024

# HERITAGE BOOKS

*AN IMPRINT OF HERITAGE BOOKS, INC.*

## Books, CDs, and more—Worldwide

For our listing of thousands of titles see our website
at
www.HeritageBooks.com

Published 2024 by
HERITAGE BOOKS, INC.
Publishing Division
5810 Ruatan Street
Berwyn Heights, MD 20740

Heritage Books by the author:
*The Ellis/Luke Family and Allied Families*
*The Griner/Flanders Family*
*The Joiner/Ryals Family*

International Standard Book Number
Paperbound: 978-0-7884-0147-3

# TABLE OF CONTENTS

# INTRODUCTION

When I started this project, it was intended only to learn who my ancestors were. I later decided to expand to the descendants of my maternal grandmother and grandfather. It was only to satisfy my curosity. When I showed my work to a few family members, they suggested that I publish a book.

My faithful and loving husband, Raymond Griner, helped me tremendously. He worked with me all the way, during research, and sometimes doing the research for me. My thanks to him. It took both of us to finish this task. I could not have done it without him.

You will find many names exactly the same. It was interesting to me, because this family had gotten separated and didn't really know each other. There were still many family members with the same names.

My grandmother, Sabrey Ryals Joiner, was left a widow at a young age with a lot of children. It seems that she had very little contact with the Joiner family and even less with her father and his family. We knew of other Joiner families living around and other Ryals families, but we didn't know we were kin to them. It was rewarding to find, at times, people we had known for years, were actually distant cousins.

There should be many more ancestors and descendants of these families. These were the ones gathered by the author. Maybe these will help you with your search. Happy hunting!

Maxine Ellis Griner

# THE JOINER FAMILY

The surname JOINER or JOYNER was first attached to one who was an expert craftsman, who did woodwork for the interior of houses, ships, and etc... by joining pieces of timber by mortise and tenon, and by panels fitted in groves, all without nails.

Among the troops that came into England with William the Conqueror in 1066 there was an 'Alan Le Joygnour' who was a chief carpenter. The descendants of this family still hold the place they then obtained, and are unchanged except for the spelling of their name.

Thomas Joyner, Sr. was born in 1619 in England. He departed from England on September 30, 1635 bound for Bermuda, aboard the ship "Dorst", John Flower, Master. He was 16 years old. Thomas settled in Isle of Wright County, Virginia, and from there he migrated to North Carolina. (Taken from, "Lists of Immigrants to America, 1600 - 1700" by Hotten.) Thomas Joyner, Sr. died in 1695.

Thomas Joyner, Sr. married but the name of his wife is unknown. His children were:

| | | | | |
|---|---|---|---|---|
| John Joyner | b. 1652 | d. 5/22/1745 | m. | |
| Thomas Joyner, Jr. | b. 1653 | d. 4/21/1708 | m. Elizabeth | |
| Bridgeman Joyner | b. 1655 | d. 1719 | m. Ann Mayo | |
| William Joyner, Sr. | b. 1658 | d. 5/21/1698 | m. Mary | |
| Theophilus Joyner | b. 1660 | d. 1/15/1724 | m. (1) Elinor Mann | |
| | | | (2) Henrietta Griffin | |

(Henrietta Griffin was the daughter of Andrew and Mary Griffin. She died 11/01/1750)

William Joyner, Sr., b. 1658 d. May 21, 1698. He was the son of Thomas Joyner, Sr. He married Mary. Her last name was unknown.

Their Children were:

| | | |
|---|---|---|
| William Joyner, Jr. | b. 1678 | d. 1739 |
| Abraham Joyner | b. 1680 | d. 07/09/1728 |
| Israel Joyner | b. 1682 | |

2

Joseph Joyner      b.1687                     m. Elizabeth Smelly 1722

(There were also 3 females. Their names are not known. A will showed the name of the boys, but not the girls.)

William Joyner, Jr. b. 1678 d. 1739. He was the son of William Joyner, Sr. and Mary. His wife is unknown.

Their child:

William Joyner, III   b. 1705     d. 10/25/1767

William Joyner, III was born 1705 in Va. and died 10/25/1767 in Southampton, Va. He was the son of William Joyner, Jr. and Mary. He married Elinor Smelly who was the daughter of Giles Smelly. (The name could have been spelled Smally.)

Children:

| | | |
|---|---|---|
| Elizabeth Joyner | b. 1728 in Southampton, Va. | m. Theophilus Underwood |
| William Joyner, IV | b. 1730 in Southampton, Va. | m. Ann Lawrence |
| Israel Joyner | b. 1732 in Southampton, Va. | m. |
| Ann Joyner | b. 1734 | m. Vick |
| Lewis Joyner | b. 1736 | |
| Moses Joyner | b. 1738 | |
| Giles Joyner | b. 1740 | |

William Joyner, IV b. 1730 d. 1777. He was the son of William Joyner, Jr. and Mary. He married Ann Lawrence on June 7, 1750. She had been married once before to Eley Eley.

The children of William Joyner, IV and Ann Lawrence are:

William W. Joyner        b. Unknown  d. 01/11/1783 m. Sealey
Jethro Joyner
Lawrence Joyner

William W. Joyner, b. unknown, d. 01/11/1783, married Sealey ?. He was the son of William Joyner, IV and Ann Lawrence (Eley). A descendant of Thomas Joyner, Sr., William W. Joyner was the earliest landowner in Nash County, N. C. He received a land grant of 180 acres in the late 1700's. How the land changed hands through the years is unknown. He died in Nash County, N. C. on January 11, 1783.

The children of William W. Joyner and his wife Sealey ?:

| Nathan Joyner | b. 1760 Nash Co., N.C. | m. (1) Sarah Ann Ricks |
| | | (2) Ann Griffin |
| Jacob Joyner | b. 1762 Nash Co., N.C. | m. Milley Eason |
| William A. Joyner | b. 1763 Nash Co., N.C. | m. Patience Ricks |
| Hardy Joyner | b. 1764 Nash Co., N.C. | m. Elizabeth |
| Burrell Joyner | b. 1766 Nash Co., N.C. | m. Omer |
| Jordan Joyner | b. 1767 Nash Co., N.C. | m. (1) Lydia Wright |
| | | (2) Elizabeth |
| Lewis Joyner | b. 1769 Nash Co., N.C. | m. |
| Cornelius Joyner | b. 1770 Nash Co., N.C. | m. Emily Leigh |
| Drewry Joyner | b. 1772 Nash Co., N.C. | m. |
| Nancy Ann Joyner | b. 1774 Nash Co., N.C. | m. Lewis Ricks |
| Mary Joyner | b. 1776 Nash Co., N.C. | m. John Barnes |
| Elizabeth Joyner | b. 1778 Nash Co., N.C. | m. John Joyner |

Jacob Joyner, b. 1762, was the son of William W. Joyner and wife Sealey ?. He married Milley Eason in Nash Co., N. C. on January 7, 1782. She was the daughter of Samuel and Edith Eason. Several of the sons of William W. Joyner sold their land and moved to the State of Georgia. Jacob was no exception. Jacob was in the 1790 census in North Carolina as being a White male over 16, with a wife, 5 males under 16, and 2 females. Jacob is in the 1800 Nash County, N. C. He received two draws in the 1805 Georgia Land Lottery in Bullock County. He had to have a wife and at least one child and be a resident of Georgia for one year to receive two draws.

The children of Jacob and Milley were:

Cornelius
(Possibly others)

Cornelius is the name that we can link with Jacob although he had more children. They could possibly have died young. Jacob is found in Pulaski County, Ga. in 1850 as 90 years old. In his household were also Mary Joiner, 50; Henry Hutto, 24; Polly Hutto, 16; and Francis Harrell, who is 50. It is not known who all these people are.

Cornelius Joiner was the son of Jacob Joiner. His wife is unknown. It is not known when he was born or when he died.

His child:

Thomas J. J. Joiner    b. 1821 in Ga. d. 1911         m. (1) Nancy Hutto
                                                       m. (2) Rebecca Reliford

Thomas James Jefferson Joiner, b. 1821 in Ga. d. 1911. He was the son of Cornelius Joiner and the grandson of Jacob Joiner. It seems the spelling of the last name changed in Nash County, N. C. Thomas J. J. Joiner was in Pulaski County, Ga. in the 1850 Census. He married Nancy Hutto in Pulaski County, Ga. on May 6, 1839. The marriage was performed by William Phelps, J. P. They later moved to Coffee County, Ga., where they raised their large family.

The Children were:

| Name | Birth | Death | Marriage |
|---|---|---|---|
| Harden Joiner | b. 2/27/1840 | d. 5/29/1922 | m. Jane Harrell |
| Jacob Joiner | b. 1839 | d. in CSA | |
| William Joiner | b. 1842 | d. in CSA | |
| Daniel Joiner | b. 1844 | d. CSA | |
| Benjamin Joiner | b. 1845 | d. 2/1898 | m. Martha Bowen |
| Sophia Joiner | b. 1846 | | |
| Thomas Joiner | b. 1848 | | |
| Nancy Jane Joiner | b. 1849 | | |
| Robert Joiner | b. 1851 | d. 1/18/1929 | m. (1) Susan (2) Elizabeth |
| Mary Joiner | b. 1852 | | |
| Allen Joiner | b. 1855 | | m. Susan Adams |
| Sarah Joiner | b. 1836 | | m. _____ Grant |

Nancy Hutto died May 7, 1871. She is buried at Carver's Cemetery in Coffee County, Ga.
Thomas J. J. Joiner married the second time to Rebecca Reliford or Rutherford on June 24,
1882 in Berrien County, Ga. It is not known where Thomas J. J. Joiner was buried.

Harden (Hardy) Joiner was born February 27, 1840 in Pulaski County, Ga. He was the son
of Thomas J. J. Joiner and Nancy Hutto. He married Jane Harrell in 1860. Jane Harrell
was born in 1847. She was the daughter of Lovett Harrell and Susan Nipper.

The children of Harden (Hardy) Joiner and Jane Harrell:

Gaines Joiner          b. 9/13/1866 d. 3/31/1948        m. (1) Georgiann Nipper
                                                            (2) Grayige
Richmond Joiner        b. 1867 Coffee Co., Ga.
Elizabeth Joiner       b.            d. 11/28/1942
Hardy Joiner, Jr.      b. 1898                           m. (1) Lizzie
                                                            (2) Sellers Hursey

Hardy Joiner, Sr. was a private in the Civil War on March 4, 1862. He was appointed 4th
Corporal in December 1863. He was wounded in the right arm in August 1864. The roll
for February 28, 1865, which was the last on file, shows him present. Pension records
show he was with command on April 8, 1865. (Muster Roll of Co. C, 50th Regiment Ga.
Volunteer Infantry, Army of Northern Va. C.S.A. Coffee County Guards.) He died May
29, 1922 and is buried in the Harrell Grove Cemetery in Coffee County, Ga. Jane Harrell
Joiner died in 1931 and is also buried in the Harrell Grove Cemetery.

Gaines Joiner, b. 9/13/1866 d. 3/31/1948, was the son of Hardy Joiner and Jane Harrell.
He married Georgiann Nipper. She was born January 15, 1869.

Their children:

Gaines Joiner, Jr.   b. 12/25/1893    d. 7/2/1965   m. Emma
William Joiner       b. 9/30/1891     d. 3/28/1932  m. Annie Waldron
Lucy Joiner          b.
Harvey (Hardy) Joiner
Charley Joiner       b. 1900          d. 8/30/1979  m. Mary Ellen Nipper
Lowe (Love) Joiner   b. 4/25/1906     d. 2/16/1982  m. Virue (Vinnie) Sears

| | | | |
|---|---|---|---|
| Mary J. Joiner | b. | | |
| Minnie Dell Joiner | b. | | m. (1) Carl Fender |
| | | | (2) ___ Richardson |
| Robert Joiner | | | m. (Lennie ) Penny Spikes |
| Ivey Joiner | | | m. Lizzie Hightower |
| Warren Joiner | b. 9/21/1912 | d. 3/7/1984 | m. Maudine Harper |

Georgiann Nipper Joiner died October 23, 1944 and was buried at Harrell Grove Cemetery in Coffee County, Ga. Gaines Joiner married Grayige (?) who was born in 1892. He died March 31, 1944 and was buried at Harrell Grove Cemetery.

William Joiner, b. September 30, 1891, was the son of Gaines Joiner and Georgiann Nipper. He married Annie Waldron, who was the daughter of Delessie L. Waldron and An Jane Waters. Annie was born November 17, 1894.

Their Children:

| | | |
|---|---|---|
| William Joiner, Jr. | | m. Polly Lee |
| Gerald Joiner | | |
| Alene Joiner | b. 2/1/1916 | m. Wilson Roberts |
| Arlene Joiner | b. 1921 | m. Lonnie Metts |
| Harvie Joiner | b. 09/05/1914 | m. Louise Harper |
| Lester Joiner | b. 1918 | |
| Melissa Joiner | | m. James Horner |

Harvie Joiner, b. September 5, 1914, was the son of William Joiner and Annie Waldron. He married Louise Harper September 12, 1935 in Irwin County, Ga. Louise was born July 5, 1915 and is the daughter of Perry Harper and Maxie Stone.

Their children:

| | | |
|---|---|---|
| Harvie Glendon Joiner | b. 2/5/1943 | m. Patricia Gaskins |
| Harold William Joiner | b. 2/6/1946 | m. Carline Howard |
| James Lamar Joiner | b. 7/15/1950 | m. Barbara Mathis |
| Joyce Joiner | b. 10/9/1947 | m. Russell Stone |

| Lounita Ann Joiner | b. 7/6/1940 | |
| Ronnie Winford Joiner | b. 9/21/1953 | m. Debra Wright |
| Gene Evelyn Joiner | b. 7/5/1936 d. 7/5/1936 | |

Harvie Glendon Joiner, born February 5, 1943, is the son of Harvie Joiner and Louise Harper. He married Patricia Gaskins. Patricia was born November 17, 1946 in Berrien County, Ga. She is the daughter of Lawton Gaskins.

The children of Harvie Glendon Joiner and Patricia Gaskins:

| Angela Joiner | b. 3/7/1964 | m. Jim |
| Brenda Joiner | b. 10/20/1965 | m. _____Stripling |
| Stephen Joiner | b. 1/16/1970 | |

Angela Joiner, born March 7, 1964 in Lowndes County, Ga., is the daughter of Harvie Glendon Joiner and Patricia Gaskins. She married Jim.

Their child:

Angia

Brenda Joiner, born October 20, 1965 in Lowndes County, Ga., is the daughter of Harvie Glendon Joiner and Patricia Gaskins. She married a Stripling.

Their children:

Brad
Another child

Stephen (Steve) Joiner, born January 16, 1970 in Lowndes County, Ga., is the son of Harvie Glendon Joiner and Patricia Gaskins. He married but his wife's name is unknown.

Their child:

Stevie Joiner

Harold Willaim Joiner, b. February 6, 1946, is the son of Harvie Joiner and Louise Harper. He married Carline Howard.

Their children:

| | |
|---|---|
| Derek William Joiner | b. 09/16/1969 |
| Blair Howell Joiner | b. 07/26/1973 |

James Lamar Joiner, b. July 15, 1950, is the son of Harvie Joiner and Louise Harper. He married Barbara Mathis. Barbara was born January 31, 1954 in Coffee County, Ga.

The children of James Lamar Joiner and Barbara Mathis:

| | |
|---|---|
| Kimberly Elaine Joiner | b. 9/6/1974 |
| Jennifer Joiner | b. 3/3/1975 |

Joyce Joiner, b. October 9, 1947, is the daughter of Harvie Joiner and Louise Harper. She married Russell Stone. They have one child:

| | |
|---|---|
| Vanna Joyce Stone | b. 6/21/1986 |

Ronnie Winford Joiner, b. September 21, 1953, is the son of Harvie Joiner and Louise Harper. He married Debra Wright, who was born July 16, 1955.

Their children are:

| | | |
|---|---|---|
| Melissa (Wright) Joiner | b. 9/17/1973 | m. Lewis Gray, Jr |
| Crystal Joiner | b. 2/23/1977 | |
| Brandi Joiner | b. 8/20/1979 | |
| Shiloh Joiner | b. 7/28/1982 | |
| Ronnie Chase Joiner | b. 1/12/1985 | |

Melissa (Wright) Joiner, born September 17, 1973, was the daughter of Debra Wright when she married Ronnie Joiner. She was raised as a daughter of Ronnie. Melissa married Lewis Gray, Jr.

9

The children of Melissa (Wright) Joiner and Lewis Gray, Jr.

Odessa V. Gray   b. 8/30/1990
Amanda L. Gray   b. 1/25/1993

Arlene Joiner, born 1921, was the daughter of William Joiner and Annie Waldron. She married Lonnie Metts.

Their children:

Bobby Metts
Earnest Metts

Lowe (Love) Joiner, born April 25, 1906, was the son of Gaines Joiner and Georgiann Nipper. He married Virue (Virnnie) Sears on May 7, 1926 in Coffee County, Ga. Virnnie was born October 4, 1910.

Their children:

Ruby Joiner                    m. Wielgus
Hiram Joiner
Albert Joiner
David Joiner    b. 10/28/1934
E. L. Joiner
Roy Joiner
Herbert Joiner

Virue (Virnnie) Sears Joiner died December 17, 1971. Lowe (Love) Joiner died February 16, 1982. They are both buried at Harrell Grove Cemetery.

Warren Joiner, born September 21, 1912 in Coffee County, Ga., was the son of Gaines Joiner and Georgiann Nipper. He married Maudine Harper. Maudine, born December 18, 1918, was the daughter of Mathias Harper and Helen Ring.

The children of Warren Joiner and Maudine Harper:

Opal Joiner
Gellet Joiner                                          m. Gay

Warren Joiner died March 7, 1984 in Coffee County, Ga. Maudine Harper Joiner died March 3, 1991. They are both buried at the Harrell Grove Baptist Church Cemetery.

Charlie (Charley) Joiner, born 1900, was the son of Gaines Joiner and Georgiann Nipper. He married Mary Ellen Nipper on April 18, 1923 in Coffee County, Ga.

Their children:

Preston Joiner                                         m. Mary Frances
Dorothy Joiner   b. 1/17/1927                          m. Fred Fowler

Charlie (Charley) Joiner died August 30, 1979. He is buried at Harrell Grove Cemetery.

Dorothy Joiner, born January 17, 1927, is the daughter of Charlie (Charley) Joiner and Mary Ellen Nipper. She married Fred Fowler. The names of their children are not known.

Nancy Jane Joiner, born 1849, was the daughter of Thomas J. J. Joiner and Nancy Hutto. She married Silas Carver on November 8, 1873. Silas Carver, born 1843 in Ware County, Ga., was the son of Samuel Carver and Sarah Penny.

The children of Nancy Jane Joiner and Silas Carver:

Infant daughter Carver        b. 10/11/1892 d. 10/11/1892
Fannie Carver                 b. 3/1882
Minnie Carver                 b. 4/1874
John R. Carver                b. 7/1888                 m. Nancy Boutwell
Thomas Carver                 b. 11/1879

Allen Joiner, b. 1855 in Ga., was the son of Thomas J. J. Joiner and Nancy Hutto. He married Susan Adams on August 1,1878 in Coffee County, Ga. Susan Adams was the daughter of Willoughby Adams and Ann Harrell.

The children of Allen Joiner and Susan Adams:

| | | |
|---|---|---|
| William Joiner | b. 9/28/1880 d. 5/2/1925 | m. Sabrey Carolina Ryals |
| Laura Elizabeth Joiner b. 11/17/1894 d. 10/20/1973 | | m. David Anderson |
| Thomas Joiner | b. 00/00/1888 | m. Polly Carver |

It is not known when Allen Joiner died or where he is buried, possibly an unmarked grave at Arnie Primitive Baptist Church. The child of William Joiner and Sabrey Ryals, Annie Bell Joiner, b. 10/20/1905, d. 2/1906, is buried there with him. Susan Adams Joiner didn't want to be buried there so she was buried with her son, William, at Mt. Union (Lax) Holiness Baptist Church.

William Joiner, b. September 28, 1880, was the son of Allen Joiner and Susan Adams. He married Sabrey Carolina Ryals on August 23, 1900 in Coffee County, Ga. Sabrey was born July 9, 1883 in Dodge County, Ga. She was the daughter of John Calvin Ryals and Roxie Rebecca Coleman.

Their Children:

| | | |
|---|---|---|
| Mose Joiner | b. 7/7/1901 d. 1/23/1935 | m. Nellie Victoria Todd |
| Willie Lee Joiner | b. 5/15/1903 d. 11/26/1986 | m. Beulah Lott |
| Annie Belle Joiner | b. 10/20/1905 d. 2/1906 | |
| Arthur Joiner | b. 11/15/1915 | m. Alice McNatt |
| Olif Joiner | b. 12/11/1912 d. 12/13/1954 | m. Plemon Hall |
| Ben Agie Joiner | b. 12/8/1908 d. 4/26/1988 | m. (1) _____ Smith (2) Roxie Elizabeth Bell |
| Elie Joiner | b. 5/3/1910 d. 8/7/1992 | m. (1) Myrtice Smith (2) Doris Jowers |
| Bithia Joiner | b. 12/1/1917 | m. George Lemuel Ellis |
| Jeff Joiner | b. 6/4/1920 | m. Willie Mae McNatt |
| Roscoe Joiner | b. 1/2/1922 d. 11/15/1992 | m. Rita Chaput |

William Joiner was a member of Mt. Union (Lax) Holiness Baptist Church. He held the office of Deacon. He died of pnemonia May 2, 1925 and was buried at Mt. Union Holiness Baptist Church Cemetery. Sabrey Ryals Joiner married a cousin of William's, T. J. Joiner, on August 7, 1930, in Berrien County, Ga. T. J. Joiner was born July 26, 1871

12

and died December 28, 1938. They were only married a short time and then separated. T. J. Joiner is also buried in Mt. Union (Lax) Holiness Baptist Church Cemetery.

Sabrey Ryals Joiner continued to be a member at Mt. Union (Lax) Holiness Baptist Church and raised her family alone. She died of a stroke at Berrien County Hospital in Berrien County, Ga. on August 17, 1974 and was buried at Mt. Union (Lax) Cemetery in Coffee County, Ga.

Laura Elizabeth Joiner was born November 17, 1894 in Coffee County, Ga. She was the daughter of Allen Joiner and Susan Adams. She married David (Dave) Anderson on May 19, 1908 in Coffee County, Ga. Dave was born May 8, 1888 .

Their Children:

| | | | |
|---|---|---|---|
| Thomas H. Anderson | b. 12/24/1915 | d. 11/26/1991 | m. Annie O'Neal |
| Johnny Anderson | b. 1913 | d. 4/30/1988 | m. Myrtle Gillespie |
| Mollie Anderson | b. 1911 | d. 3/12/1987 | m. Richard Metts |

Thomas H. Anderson was the son of Laura Elizabeth Joiner and David Anderson. He was born December 24, 1915. He married Annie O'neal on October 15, 1933 in Coffee County, Ga. Annie was born August 27, 1917, the daughter of Willis O'Neal and Hazel Mae Ledon. Thomas (Tom) became a deacon at Willacoochee Holiness Baptist Church for several years before he moved his membership.

The children of Thomas H. Anderson and Annie O'Neal:

| | | |
|---|---|---|
| Burnell Anderson | b. 9/15/1935 | m. Ruby Hall |
| Doris Anderson | b. 10/8/1943 | m. (1) Edsel Harper |
| | | (2) J. W. Roberts |
| | | (3) Edsel Harper |
| | | (4) Robert (Bob) Shatto |
| | | (5) Bobby Hall |
| | | (6) Roger Mills |
| | | (7) Roy Yancey |
| Verneil Anderson | b. 11/12/1953 | m. (1) Wayne Sweat |
| | | (2) Chester Hall |

Tom Anderson and Annie separated. Tom married again but her name is not known. Annie married the second time to Emory M. Rowell on May 30, 1980 in Coffee County, Ga.

Tom died November 26, 1991 and is buried at Mt. Union (Lax) Holiness Baptist Church Cemetery.

Burnell Anderson, b. September 15, 1935, is the son of Thomas H. Anderson and Annie O'Neal. He married Ruby Hall on January 26, 1956 in Coffee County, Ga. Ruby Hall, born November 9, 1939, is the daughter of Glenn Hall and Lois Marie Steverson.

The children of Burnell and Ruby Hall Anderson:

| Angelia Marie Anderson | b. 3/27/1957 | m. Ronnie Batten |
| Donna Kay Anderson | b. 4/19/1958 | m. Kenneth O'Steen |

Angelia Marie Anderson, born March 27, 1957, is the daughter of Burnell Anderson and Ruby Hall. She married Ronnie Batten.

The children of Angelia Marie Anderson and Ronnie Batten:

| Amy Miranda Batten | b. 7/19/1977 |
| Benjah Batten, III | b. 11/19/1979 |

Donna Kay Anderson, born April 19, 1958, is the daughter of Burnell Anderson and Ruby Hall. She married Kenneth O'Steen.

Their children:

| Kendra Leigh O'Steen | b. 9/15/1978 |
| Kacie Amanda O'Steen | b. 4/8/1981 |

Doris Anderson, born October 8, 1943, is the daughter of Thomas H. Anderson and Annie O'Neal. She married Edsel Harper.

14

The children of Doris Anderson and Edsel Harper:

| | | | |
|---|---|---|---|
| Jean Harper | b. | m. | Ed Shatto |
| Retha Dean Harper | b. 12/20/1960 | m. | Darrell Horton |
| James Horace Harper | b. 07/16/1962 | m. | Kathy Merritt |

Doris Anderson, born October 8, 1943 and daughter of Thomas H. Anderson and Annie O'Neal, married the second time to J. W. Roberts.

Their child:

| | | |
|---|---|---|
| Ricky Roberts | b. | m. |

Doris Anderson, b. October 8, 1943, married her first husband, Edsel Harper, the third time. She married the fourth time to Robert Shatto.

Their children:

| | | | |
|---|---|---|---|
| Robert Shatto, Jr. | b. | m. | Jeana Mancil |
| Sharon Shatto | b. | m. | Buddy Bennett |
| Cynthia Shatto | b. 7/21/1968 | m. | Robbie Grantham |

Doris Anderson, born October 8, 1943, married the fifth time to Bobby Hall. There were no children by him. She married the sixth time to Roger Mills and they had no children. She married the seventh time to Roy Yancey.

Jean Harper, b. , is the daughter of Doris Anderson and Edsel Harper. She married Ed Shatto.

Their children:

Michelle Shatto
Son
Son

Retha Dean Harper, born December 20, 1960, is the daughter of Doris Anderson and Edsel Harper. She married Darrell Horton. Darrell was born August 22, 1958.

Their children:

| | |
|---|---|
| Laura M. Horton | b. 5/4/1978 |
| Darrell A. Horton | b. 9/11/1979 |
| Kelly M. Horton | b. 4/28/1981 |
| Hedi Horton | b. 11/12/1982 |
| Danny T. Horton | b. 2/19/1985 |
| Mathew D. Horton | b. 4/18/1990 |
| Amanda L. Horton | b. 4/10/1992 |

James Horace Harper, born July 16, 1962, is the son of Doris Anderson and Edsel Harper. He married Kathy A. Merritt. Kathy was born November 6, 1964.

Their children:

| | |
|---|---|
| James E. Harper | b. 1/4/1984 |
| Jessica R. Harper | b. 10/17/1992 |

Cynthia Shatto, born July 21, 1968, is the daughter of Doris Anderson and Robert Shatto. She married Robbie Grantham. He was born October 10, 1962.

Their child:

Dawn Grantham      b.

Robert Shatto, Jr., born      , is the son of Doris Anderson and Robert Shatto, Sr. He married Jeana Mancil.

Their children:

Child Shatto      b.
Child Shatto      b.

Sharon Shatto, born unknown, is the daughter of Doris Anderson and Robert Shatto, Sr. She married Buddy Bennett.

Their child:

Child Bennett        b.

Verneil Anderson, b. November 12, 1953, in Coffee County, Ga., is the daughter of Thomas H. Anderson and Annie O'Neal. She married first Wayne Sweat on November 6, 1969.

Their children:

| Thomas W. Sweat | b. 2/8/1973 | m. (1) Laura Jo Mancil |
| | | (2) Jennifer Duggan Mathis |
| Crystal Laneil Sweat | b. 3/3/1976 | |
| Kacey DaNean Sweat | b. 9/24/1980 | |
| Brandi Leigh Sweat | b. 5/14/1983 | |

Crystal Laneil Sweat, born March 3, 1976, is the daughter of Verneil Anderson and Wayne Sweat. She has a daughter.

Keety Shiann Sweat        b. 2/14/1994

Verneil Anderson married the second time to Chester Hall on January 14, 1991. They have no children.

Johnnie Anderson, born 1913, was the son of Laura Elizabeth Joiner and David Anderson. He married Myrtle Gillespie on June 1, 1939 in Coffee County, Ga.

Their children:

Roger Anderson
Robert Anderson
David Anderson

| Elaine Anderson | m. Day |
| Linda Anderson | m. Edgerton |
| LaRue Anderson | m. Meeks |

Johnnie Anderson died April 30, 1988 in Ware County, Ga. He is buried at Chatterton Holiness Baptist Church Cemetery where he was a member.

Mollie Anderson, born 1911, was the daughter of Laura Elizabeth Joiner and David Anderson. She married Richard Metts.

Their children:

| Dot Metts | m. Howell |
| Pat Metts | m. Hickox |

Mollie's husband preceeded her in death. She died March 12, 1987 in Jacksonville, Fla. She is buried in the Greenlawn Cemetery in Waycross, Ga.

Thomas Joiner, born 1888 in Ga., was the son of Allen Joiner and Susan Adams. He married Polly Carver April 7, 1907 in Coffee County, Ga. Polly was the daughter of Needham Carver and Amanda Thomas.

The child of Thomas Joiner and Polly Carver:

Walter Joiner     b. 11/3/1910 d. 12/25/1960   m. Lucy Merritt

Walter Joiner, b. November 3, 1910, was the son of Thomas Joiner and Polly Carver. He married Lucy Merritt on November 10, 1929 in Coffee County, Ga. Lucy was born February 23, 1914.

Their children:

| Vivian Joiner | b. 5/27/19? | m. Chester Lankford |
| Wilbert Joiner | b. 8/18/1932 | m. Mae Leslie |
| Aubrey Joiner | b. 9/9/1934 | m. Jeannette Adams |

Lorene Joiner  b. 10/28/1938   m. Bernie Fussell
Orvel Joiner   b. 9/18/1941 d. 9/18/1941

Walter died December 25, 1960. He is buried at Vickers Rural Cemetery. Lucy Merritt died July 7, 1991 and is also buried at Vickers Rural Cemetery in Coffee County, Ga.

Wilbert Joiner, born August 18, 1932, is the son of Walter Joiner and Lucy Merritt. He married Mae Leslie on January 5, 1962 in Coffee County, Ga.

The children of Wilbert Joiner and Mae Leslie:

Teresa Ann Joiner  b. 10/5/1962   m. Charles Guernsey
Cheryl Joiner   b. 1/16/1965   m. Ronnie Solomon
Roy Dale Joiner  b. 8/4/1968    m. Angela Hope

Aubrey Joiner, born September 9, 1934, is the son of Walter Joiner and Lucy Merritt. He married Jeannette Adams.

Their children:

Mitchell Thompson
Walter Lee Joiner
Janice Jessica Joiner

Lorene Joiner, born October 28, 1938, is the daughter of Walter Joiner and Lucy Merritt. She married Bernie Fussell.

The children of Lorene Joiner and Bernie Fussell:

Lamar Fussell    b. 1/5/1958
Twyla Elaine Fussell b. 9/14/1959   m. Troy David Carter

Twyla Elaine Fussell, born September 14, 1959, is the daughter of Bernie Fussell and Lorene Joiner. She married Troy David Carter.

The children of Twyla Elaine Fussell and Troy David Carter:

Dustin Grant Carter
Troy David Carter, Jr.
Joshua Todd Carter

Vivian Joiner, born May 27,     , is the daughter of Walter Joiner and Lucy Merritt. She married Chester Lankford. They have four children. Their names are unknown.

## ROYAL/RYAL FAMILY

The name "Royal" has been spelled and recorded in many ways: Royall, Royals, Royle, Rohle, Ryals, and Ryall to name a few. All are descendants of the Norman Ancestor, Turston Due Roi. In ancient and medieval time, the Du roi (French for Royall) family occupied a baronage on the west bank of the River Seine, in Normandy. They were powerful figures in the political and economical life of the province under William, Duke of Normandy. They were listed as accompanying William the Conqueror in the invasion of England in 1066.

The American branch of the family comes from the immigrant Joseph Royall, who came from England aboard the ship "Charitie" July, 1622. He was living at "Ye Neak of Land," February 16, 1623.

Joseph Royall was born in England around 1600. His father was William Royall also born in England about 1570.

Joseph Royall was at "Charles Cittie," February 24, 1624. He was married before 1637, first, Thomassia _____; second, Ann _____; third, about 1645, Katherine Banks.

Virginia Patent Books I, II, III show 1100 acres of land granted by the king for transportation of twenty persons into the colony, many of whom were of well known families. Location was Turkey Creek, Diggs Hundred, and on the James River above Shirley Hundred. Since 1637, part of this land has been in possession of descendants, the ancestral home known as Doghams, said to be a variation of some French name of a stream in Normandy. According to Brock, Royalls, and old wax seals on Virginia records, there was a coat of arms.

Joseph Royall married Katherine Banks around 1645. She was born around 1625. Their children were:

| | | | |
|---|---|---|---|
| Joseph Royall | b. 1646 | m. | Mary Epps |
| Sarah Royall | b. | m. | John Wilkinson |
| Katherine Royall | b. | m. | (1) ____Farrar |
| | | | (2) Richard Perrin |

| (Daughter) Royall | b. | m. | _____ Dennis |
| (Daughter) Royall | b. | m. | _____ Maschell |

Joseph Royall died about 1658 in Virginia and his wife, Katherine married Henry Isham.
They had one son, Henry Isham, Jr. He never married. Katherine died around 1686.
There was never a will found for Joseph Royall but there was a will for Katherine and her
son Henry Isham, Jr. According to the will, there were other children by Henry Isham.
They were: Mary Isham, who married William Randolph and Ann, who married Francis
Epps.

Joseph Royall, b. 1646, was the son of Joseph Royall and Katherine Banks. He was a
Captain and was referred to as Captain Joseph Royall. Virginia Patent Books 7, 8, 9, 10
and Henrico records show Captain Joseph Royall had for himself and in connection with
Col. William Randolph, Col. Francis Eppes, and George Archer, 4,542 acres of land,
embracing Martin's Swamp on the south side of the James River, and on Proctor's Creek.
His title, service as sheriff, and as vestryman in Curl's Episcopal Church, and innumerable
references to him in public documents enable us to know much about him and his heirs. Up
to now no will has been found.

Capt. Joseph Royall married Mary Eppes around 1681 in Virginia. Mary Eppes was born
in 1664, the daughter of Col. Francis Eppes and Elizabeth Littleberry.

Their children were:

| Joseph Royall, Jr. | b. 1681 | | m. Elizabeth Kennon |
| William Royall | b. 1688 | | m. Sarah Povall |
| Henry Royall | b. Unknown | | m. (1) Unknown |
| | | | (2) Mary (wid. of George Archer) |
| Sarah Royall | b. Unknown | | Probably never married |
| Joseph Royall | b. Unknown | d. around 1732 | |

William Royall, b. 1688 was the son of Captain Joseph and Mary Eppes Royall. He
married Sarah Povall, daughter of Robin Povall and Elizabeth Hooker.

The children of William Royall and Sarah Povall:

| | | |
|---|---|---|
| William Royall | b. before 1728 | m. Elizabeth |
| Joseph Royall | b. | m. Peninah |
| John Royall | b. between 1720 - 1730 | m. Susanna Bates |
| Sarah Royall | b. | m. Nathaniel Terry before 1760 |

William Royall, born before 1728, was the son of William Royall and Sarah Povall. His wife's name was Elizabeth. It is not known what her maiden name was.

Their children were:

William Ryals   b. 02/01/1748  d. 02/01/1828          m. Edith Childs
Joseph Ryals
John Ryals

William Ryals, born February 1, 1748, was the son of William Royall and Elizabeth. He was born in North Carolina. The spelling of the name was changed in North Carolina. He married Edith Childs, who was born 1755. They moved to Georgia the latter part of the 18th century and settled in Montgomery County.

William Ryals was a Revolutionary Soldier and served as a Private in Armstrong's 2nd North Carolina Regiment. He died on February 1, 1828 and is buried in the Dead River Cemetery twelve miles south of Mt. Vernon, Montgomery County, Ga. His grave is marked by the Daughters of the American Revolution. His will was probated March 3, 1828. (See Book A. Record of Wills, Montgomery County, Ga. pages 270-273) Edith died 1835 in Montgomery County, Ga.

William and Edith's children were:

| | | |
|---|---|---|
| William Ryley Ryals | b. 1799 | m. (1) Eliza Conner |
| | | (2) Charlotte Clark |
| Joseph Ryals | b. 11/20/1796 d. 9/8/1859 | m. Lucy Ann Conner |
| Winnifred Ryals | b. 1786        d. 7/13/1863 | m. Angres Calhoun |
| Mary Ann Ryals | | m. Thomas Hall |
| Elizabeth Ryals | | m. _____ Womack |
| Penelope Ryals | b. 9/11/1798 d. 3/15/1844 | m. James Gassaway Conner |

Matilda Ryals        b. 12/26/1800 d. 1/20/1886  m. Robert Partin
John Bryan Ryals     b. 1/28/1809  d. 6/2/1863   m. (1) Marie McDonald Conner
                                                     (2) Frances Ellen Wall

William Ryley Ryals, born 1799 in Sampson County, N. C., was the son of William Ryals
(R.S.) and Edith Childs. He lived in North Carolina with his family until they moved to
Montgomery County Georgia around 1807. They lived in Tattnall County and Montgomery
County until around 1860. He married Eliza Conner on February 22, 1828 in Montgomery
County. She was born around 1803. Her parents were Rev. Wilson Connor and Mary
Cook.

William Ryley Ryals and Eliza's children:

Maria Ryals          b.                    m. _____Clements
Jane Ryals           b.                    m. (1) _____McAllister
                                              (2) Bud Adams
Lucy Ann Ryals       b. 1829              m. Newton Nash
Eliza Elizabeth Ryals b. Unknown   d. in infancy

Eliza Conner died September 1, 1831 in Montgomery County. She was only 28 years old.
She is buried in the Dead River Cemetery.

William Ryley Ryals then married Charlotte Clark.  Charlotte was born on December 5,
1809. She was the daughter of Elijah Clark, Jr. and Margaret Long. She and William
Ryley Ryals married somewhere around 1832.  They had the following children:

Joshua Ryals         b. 1833      d. 10/6/1862 CSA    m. Susan Adams
Thomas Ryals         b. 1835      d. after 1890       m. Ann Jane Burch
William G. Ryals     b. 1837      d. ? CSA            m. Mary Henderson
Joseph Ryals         b. 1845
Eliza Ryals          b. 1/29/1848 d. 1/13/1938        m. Charles Purvis
Orren (Oren) Ryals   b. 1851                          m. (1) Rebecca Mills
                                                         (2) Bertha
John Calvin Ryals    b. 10/26/1854 d. 9/4/1912        m. Roxie Rebecca Coleman

William Ryley Ryals died May 4, 1863 in Montgomery County, Ga. of pneumonia, while visiting a brother. He was buried in the Dead River Cemetery in Montgomery County. His residence was in Clinch County, Ga. at the time he died. His widow, Charlotte Clark Ryals died March 7, 1885 and was buried in the Union Hill Cemetery.

Lucy Ann Ryals, born 1829, was the daughter of William Riley Ryals and Eliza Conner. She married Newton Nash on January 23, 1853. Newton Nash, born 1827, was the son of James Nash and Sarah Whitehurst.

Their children:

| | | |
|---|---|---|
| Olive (Oliff M.) Nash | b. 1/25/1854 d. 8/17/1939 | m. Martin Jasper Griner |
| Mariah L. Nash | b. 1855 | |
| Mary Jane Nash | b. 1857 | |
| Alif L.Nash | b. 1861 | |
| John W. Nash | b. 1863 | |
| Ann Eliza Nash | b. 1866 | |
| James Nash | b. 1868 | |

Lucy Ann Ryals died before 1871, because Newton Nash was married to Mary Griffin, born 1844, the daughter of James Griffin, on March 6, 1871.

Olive (Oliff M.) Nash, born January 25, 1854 in Montgomery County, Ga., was the daughter of Lucy Ann Ryals and Newton Nash. The family had moved to Berrien County, Ga. in 1868. She married Martin Jasper Griner on December 11, 1859. Martin was born August 27, 1842, the son of Daniel Griner and Rebecca Strickland.

Their children:

| | | |
|---|---|---|
| Jasper M. Griner | b. 1/16/1873 d. 11/23/1946 | |
| Ida C. Griner | b. 12/22/1874 d. 11/6/1957 | m. _____ Ross |
| Daniel Newton Griner | b. 6/4/1877 d. 12/6/1961 | m. Anna Bradford |
| Oliver C. Griner | b. 9/1879 | |
| Edna Eleanor Griner | b. 5/11/1882 d. 6/19/1939 | m. _____ Harris |
| Robert Bruce Griner | b. 5/1884 d. about 1980-81 | |

| Ernest C. Griner | b. 8/1889 | |
| Adlai B. Griner | b. 2/1892 | |
| Agnes Virginia Griner | b. | m. W. R. Futch |

Martin Jasper Griner died August 12, 1914 and Olive Nash Griner died August 17, 1939. They are both buried in the Old Nashville Cemetery in Nashville, Ga.

Daniel Newton Griner, born June 4, 1877, was the son of Martin Jasper Griner and Olive Nash. He married Anna Bradford, daughter of Thomas Bradford. She was born February 14, 1877.

Their children:

Vera Griner
Annie Laura Griner
F. P. Griner
Mamie Griner

Daniel Newton Griner died December 6, 1961. His wife, Anna, died February 19, 1952 They are both buried at Pleasant Cemetery.

Robert Bruce Griner, born May 1884, was the son of Martin Jasper Griner and Olive Nash. He died about 1980 or 1981.

His children:

| Dorothy Griner | m. Ward or Pritchett |
| Carmen Griner | m. Stone |
| Robert W. Griner | |
| Frances Griner | m. Miley |
| Sarah Griner | m. Norman |
| Fairy Griner | m. Powell |
| James Hasty Griner | |

Agnes Virginia Griner, born unknown, was probably the daughter of Martin Jasper Griner and Olive Nash. She married W. R. Futch on April 26, 1892.

The children of Agnes Virginia Griner and W. R. Futch:

Dobbin Futch
Otis Futch
Pearl Futch
Governor Futch

Orren (Oren) Ryals was the son of William Ryley Ryals and Charlotte Clark. He was born July 12, 1850 in Mt. Vernon, Ga. He married Rebecca Ann Mills on October 25, 1871. Rebecca Ann was the daughter of Mary Sears and her father was a Mills.

Their children:

| | | |
|---|---|---|
| Joshua C. Ryals | b. 8/15/1872 Clinch Co., Ga. | m. Elizabeth Cornelia Taylor February 22, 1895 |
| Mollie Elizabeth Ryals | b. 7/23/1873 | m. Solomon Sears |
| Tilitha Ryals | b. | m. H. I Brown |

Orren (Oren) Ryals married the second time to Bertha. Her maiden name is unknown. He died October 8, 1920 in Cornelia, Ga.

Mollie Elizabeth Ryals, b. July 23, 1873, was the daughter of Orren (Oren) Ryals and Rebecca Ann Mills. She married Solomon Sears. He was the son of Hamilton Sears and Mary (Polly) Vickers.

Their children:

| | | | |
|---|---|---|---|
| Tabitha Sears | b. 10/30/1893 | d. 6/20/1973 | m. David Carter |
| Rebecca Sears | b. 4/2/1895 | | m. Fred J. Brown |
| Hansel V. Sears | b. 2/1/1897 | d. 1/5/1994 | m. Queen Victoria Tanner |
| Stanford Sears | b. 1/13/1906 | d. 12/14/1969 | m. Margaret McMillan |
| Eunice (Una) Sears | b. 11/11/? | | m. Osbon J. Mills |
| Floy Sears | b. 6/7/? | | m. John W. Roberts |
| Bryan Sears | b. 11/26/1901 | d. 1/26/1902 | |

Solomon Sears died August 8, 1936 in Coffee County, Ga. It is not known where he was buried. His widow, Mollie Elizabeth Ryals Sears died December 5, 1955. She is buried in the Franklin Holiness Baptist Church Cemetery in Coffee County, Ga.

Tabitha Sears, born October 30, 1893, was the daughter of Mollie Elizabeth Ryals and Solomon Sears. She married David Carter who was the son of William Carter and Manassa Kirkland. He was born September 15, 1890.

The children of Tabitha Sears and David Carter:

Hubert Carter
Sol Carter
Paul E. Carter
Lois Carter                    m. Jimmy Stevens
Maggie Carter                  m. Gibson
Opal Carter                    m. Medders
Floye Carter                   m. Williams
Lizzie Carter                  m. Mancil
Lula Carter                    m. Robert Taylor
Ruth Carter                    m. Lindsey Brigmon

Tabitha Sears died June 20, 1973 in Jacksonville, Fla. David Carter died July 2, 1953. They are both buried in the Franklin Holiness Baptist Cemetery in Douglas, Ga.

Hansel Vernon Sears, born February 1, 1897, was the son of Mollie Elizabeth Ryals and Solomon Sears. He married Queen Victoria Tanner on July 15, 1917.

Their children:

| | | |
|---|---|---|
| Vollie Sears | b. 5/15/1924  d. 11/5/1987 | m. Elizabeth Batten |
| Ruby Sears | b. | m. Hiram (Buster) Davis, Jr. |
| Mollie Sears | b. | m. Hubert McKinnon |

Hansel Vernon Sears was a retired minister with the Holiness Baptist Association. He had been in the ministry for approximately 50 years, before his retirement. He died at the age of 96 on January 5, 1994. His was survived by his wife of 75 years.

Vollie Sears, born May 16, 1924, was the son of Rev. Hansel Vernon Sears and Queen Victoria Tanner. He married Elizabeth Batten.

Their child:

Bobby Sears

Mollie Sears, born unknown, is the daughter of Rev. Hansel Vernon Sears and Queen Victoria Tanner. She married Hubert McKinnon.

Their children:

Jessie McKinnon
Patsy McKinnon                          died at age of 6

Ruby Sears, born unknown, was the daughter of Rev. Hansel Sears and Queen Victoria Tanner. She married Hiram (Buster) Davis, Jr.

Their children:

Dean Davis                              m. Brown
Dale Davis                              m. Ralph Tanner

Stanford Sears, born January 13, 1906, died December 14, 1969, was the son of Mollie Elizabeth Ryals and Solomon Sears. He married Margaret McMillan, born September 30, 1905, died May 28, 1988. She was the daughter of Daniel "Babe" McMillan and Pink Purvis. She was buried at the Satilla Memorial Gardens.

Their children:

James Bryan Sears        b. 5/29/1929      m. Willie Mae Carver McDonald
Dorothy Lucille Sears    b. 10/19/1931     m. Bradley Felton Cliett, Jr.

Nellie Francis Sears   b. 1/17/1934            m. Carl Hendrick Chaires
Helen Jeanette Sears   b. 7/6/1936   d. 5/4/1987   m. Herman Sheldon Henderson
Geraldine Sears         b. 5/5/1939            m. (1) Curtis Purvis
                                              (2) James Howard Johnson, Jr.
Charles Hampton Byrd  b. 3/21/1948 (Adopted)

James Bryan Sears, born May 29, 1929, is the son of Stanford Sears and Margaret McMillan. He married Willie Mae Carver McDonald who was born on February 24, 1933.

Their children:

Cynthia Ann Sears      b. 6/2/1952            m. Arthur P. Snipes, Jr.
Hattie Elaine Sears    b. 11/1955   d. 2/14/1957
James Bryan Sears, Jr. b. 3/13/1961           m. Terri Lee Griffin

Cynthia Ann Sears, born June 2, 1952, is the daughter of James Bryan Sears and Willie Mae Carver McDonald. She married Arthur P. Snipes, Jr.

Their children:

Scott Bryan Snipes     b. 8/1/1973
Eric Wayne Snipes      b. 5/8/1976
John Austin Snipes     b. 1/12/1978

Dorothy Lucille Sears, born October 19, 1931, is the daughter of Stanford Sears and Margaret McMillan. She married Bradley Felton Cliett, Jr. He was born December 31, 1923.

Their children:

Bradley Felton Cliett, III   b. 12/18/1951      m. Lois Thompson
Angela Cliett                b. 4/19/1954       m. Earl S. Carter
Donald Cliett (Twin)         b. 4/27/1955
Deborah Cliett (Twin)        b. 4/27/1955
Marcus Stanford Cliett       b. 1/24/1958       m. Diane Burnett

Bradley Felton Cliett, III, born December 18, 1951, is the son of Dorothy Lucille Sears and Bradley Felton Cliett, Jr. He married Lois Thompson. She was born March 16, 1949.

The children of Bradley Felton Cliett, III and Lois Thompson:

Temple Ann Thompson      b. 7/18/1969
Bonita Thompson          b. 7/23/1972
Bradley Felton Cliett, IV  b. 6/16/1976

Angela Cliett, born April 19, 1954, is the daughter of Dorothy Lucille Sears and Bradley Felton Cliett, Jr. She married Earl S. Carter. He was born January 7, 1949.

Their children:

Christy Elaine Carter     b. 8/14/1973
Michael Earl Carter       b. 8/6/1975
Marci Denise Carter       b. 3/16/1984

Marcus Stanford Cliett, born January 24, 1958, died April 6, 1983, was the son of Dorothy Lucille Sears and Bradley Felton Cliett, Jr. He married Diane Burnett.

Their children:

Amanda Lee Cliett   b. 5/16/1981
Julie Marie Cliett  b. 1/17/1983

Nellie Francis Sears, born January 17, 1934, is the daughter of Stanford Sears and Margaret McMillan. She married Carl Hendrick Chaires. Carl was born January 16, 1935.

Their children:

Margaret Ann Chaires    b. 9/26/1958      m. Don Johnson
Carl David Chaires      b. 11/18/1961
Kenneth Wayne Chaires   b. 11/28/1965

Margaret Ann Chaires, born September 26, 1958, is the daughter of Nellie Francis Sears and Carl Hendrick Chaires. She married Don Johnson. Don was born September 11, 1957.

The children of Margaret Ann Chaires and Carl Hendrick Chaires:

| | |
|---|---|
| Lauren Michelle Johnson | b. 2/2/1984 |
| Carly Jeanette Johnson | b. 9/8/1987 |

Carl David Chaires, born November 18, 1961, is the son of Nellie Francis Sears and Carl Hendrick Chaires. He is not married but has two children.

His children:

| | |
|---|---|
| Ashley Adelle Chaires | b. 8/30/1983 |
| Justin Carl Chaires | b. 9/11/1984 |

Helen Jeanette Sears, born July 6, 1936, died May 4, 1987, was the daughter of Stanford Sears and Margaret McMillan. She married Herman Sheldon Henderson. He was born January 13, 1935.

Their children:

| | | |
|---|---|---|
| Deborah Elaine Henderson | b. 3/13/1957 | m. Alan Dougald McLarty |
| Pamela Margarette Henderson | b. 6/23/1962 | m. Bruce Patrick Thomas |

Deborah Elaine Henderson, born March 13, 1957, is the daughter of Helen Jeanette Sears and Herman Sheldon Henderson. She married Alan Dougald McLarty. He was born January 24, 1958.

Their children:

| | |
|---|---|
| Stephanie Elaine McLarty | b. 5/27/1984 |
| Allison Jeanette McLarty | b. 1/13/1989 |

Pamela Margaret Henderson, born June 23, 1962, is the daughter of Helen Jeanette Sears and Herman Sheldon Henderson. She married Bruce Patrick Thomas. He was born August 11, 1959.

The children of Pamela Margaret Henderson and Bruce Patrick Thomas:

Marshall Patrick Thomas    b. 8/21/1985
Jesse Helen Thomas    b. 10/27/1988

Geraldine Sears, born May 5, 1939, is the daughter of Stanford Sears and Margaret McMillan. She married Curtis Purvis and then James Howard Johnson, Jr. James was born May 6, 1944.

Her children:

Gary Dewayne Purvis    b. 12/29/1961    m. Donna Lynn Spell
Sherrie Moore    b. 10/25/1962
Mitchell Moore    b. 08/17/1964
Marcia Lynn Johnson    b. 8/6/1966

Gary Dewayne Purvis, born December 29, 1961, is the son of Geraldine Sears and Curtis Purvis. He married Donna Lynn Spell. She was born October 12, 1964.

Their child:

Michael Lee Purvis    b. 5/8/1981

John Calvin Ryals, born October 24, 1854 in Coffee County, Ga., was the son of William Ryley Ryals and Charlotte Clark. He married Roxie Rebecca Coleman on August 22, 1875 in Dodge County, Ga. The wedding was performed by J. T. Kinchen. Her parents were William Andrew Coleman and Priscilla Wright. Roxie was born on February 24, 1855 in Dodge County, Ga.

Their children:

Irene (Iriney) Ryals    b. 12/7/1879 d. 12/27/1975 m. Elias Metts

| Hattie (Hariette) Ryals | b. 3/27/1892 | d. 1/18/1976 | m. (1) Wiley Ellis |
| | | | (2) Wiley Hutcheson |
| Beadie Ann Ryals | b. 10/19/1888 | d. 11/1945 | m. (1) J. Bowen 8/4/1904 |
| | | | (2) Andrew Stewart |
| Nancy Elizabeth Ryals | b. 2/7/1880 | d. 12/2/1950 | m. Raymond Carver |
| Henry Melvin Ryals | b. 10/10/1896 | d. 11/6/1952 | m. Elma R. Chappell |
| Sabrey Carolina Ryals | b. 7/9/1883 | d. 8/17/1974 | m. (1) William Joiner |
| | | | (2) T. J. Joiner |
| Joel Wilson Ryals | b. 11/14/1884 | d. 2/10/1969 | m. Bessie M. Royals |
| Mary Jane (Mollie) Ryals | b. 6/9/1876 | d. | m. Elias Jack Guest |
| William Riley Ryals | b. 5/7/1877 | d. 3/14/1878 | |
| Wade Joshuaway Ryals | b. 1/9/1879 | d. 9/17/1880 | |
| Emmer Percilla Ryals | b. 4/15/1892 | d. 9/16/1896 | |
| James Calvin Ryals | b. 8/22/1886 | d. 11/16/1887 | |

The story was told by Sabrey Carolina Ryals Joiner that her father was a mean man. He put her mother in Millegeville State Mental Hospital and left her there. She always felt that her mother was not insane but at that time whatever a man decided to do to his wife was allowed. No one interferred, not even her family. Roxie died in Millegeville Hospital March, 1908, and is buried in Dodge County, probably in the Coleman family cemetery.

John Calvin Ryals died September 4, 1912 in Coffee County, Ga. It is not known where he is buried.

(Sabrey Carolina Ryals and William Joiner had a large family. They are listed in the Decendants of William Joiner and Sabrey Carolina Ryals Family section.)

Mary Jane (Mollie) Ryals, born June 9, 1876, was the daughter of John Calvin Ryals and Roxie Rebecca Coleman. She married Elias Jack Guest on July 3, 1892 in Coffee County, Ga. Jack Guest was born August, 1874.

Their children:

Polly Ann Guest     b. 9/1893

Maude Estelle Guest  b. 5/1896          m. Plageman
Nancy Guest          b. 2/1899

Maude Estelle Guest, born May, 1896, was the daughter of Mary Jane (Mollie) Ryals and Elias Jack Guest. She married _____ Plageman.

The child of Maude Estelle Guest and Plageman:

Fred Plageman

Nancy Elizabeth Ryals, born February 7, 1880, was the daughter of John Calvin Ryals and Roxie Rebecca Coleman. She married Raymond Carver on June 13, 1895. Raymond Carver, born August 2, 1877, was the son of Sampson "Braz" Brazwell Carver and Sallie (Sarah) Davis.

Their children:

Olive Maybel Carver     b. 7/13/1897 d. 8/8/1898
Brazien (Brazie) Carver  b. 12/12/1898          m. Fannie Alene Stevens
Dennis Wesley Carver     b. 10/9/1900 d. 6/9/1957  m. Mary Delree Tyner
Leroy Carver             b. 11/29/1901          m. (1) Estell Holton
                                                    (2) Ida Mae Walker

Mary Jane (Mollie) Carver b. 11/13/1904          m. Theodore Hubert Strickland
Anna Belle Carver        b. 4/26/1908           m. Early Johnson Carter
Estelle Carver           b. 5/18/1910           m. (1) James Harley Ray
                                                    (2) Antone Hutchison Wells
                                                    (3) Morris Garrett

Winnie Grace Carver      b. 3/20/1902           m. Ocie C. Carter
Johnnie Brazie Carver    b. 5/6/1903 d. 1/1905
Joseph Carver            b. 9/18/1906 d. 7/1908
Raymond Carver Jr.       b. 4/12/1914 d. 4/26/1914
Melvin Ryals Carver      b. 10/11/1917 d. at birth

Raymond Carver died December 10, 1946 and his wife, Nancy Ryals Carver, died December 4, 1950. They are both buried in the Carver Church Cemetery.

Brazien (Brazie) Carver, born December 12, 1898 in Coffee County, Ga., the son of Nancy Elizabeth Ryals and Raymond Carver. He is the second child and eldest son. His oldest sister, Olive Mabel, died shortly before he was born. He was named for his Uncle Bazeen, who was named after a famous French Marshall named Bazaine. The name was later changed to Bazie. He married Fannie Alene Stevens.

Joel Wilson Ryals, born November 14, 1884, was the son of John Calvin Ryals and Roxie Rebecca Coleman. He married Bessie Royals on October 4, 1908, according to the Coffee County Marriages. The family bible states they were married on November 18, 1908.

Bessie was born April 24, 1891. She refused to name her children Ryals. She felt the name should be Royals and that is exactly how she spelled their names.

The children of Joel Wilson Ryals and Bessie Royals:

Clayton Royals      b. 6/6/2929  d. 3/29/1992  m. Ethel Davis
Clarence Royals     b. 3/14/1911 d. 5/7/1989   m. Eileen Ricketson
Wilson Royals       b. 6/18/1913 d. 7/5/1981   m. Audice Wright
Annie Belle Royals  b. 7/18/1909 d. 10/24/1943 m. (1) J. C. Sweats
                                                  (2) _____ Benefield
Elton Royals        b. 8/29/1925 d. 9/30/1992  m. Mary Nell Silas
Joel William Royals b. 4/24/1921 d. 4/14/1994  m. Alma Morgan

Bessie Royals died September 14, 1958 in Atkinson County, Ga. She is buried in Mt. Pleasant Cemetery. Joel Wilson Ryals died February 10, 1969 in Coffee County, Ga. He is buried in Mt. Pleasant Cemetery.

Clayton Royals, born June 6, 1919, was the son of Joel Wilson Ryals and Bessie Royals. He married Ethel Davis on September 5, 1942. Ethel's parents were Henry Davis and Allie Bell Lairsey.

The children of Clayton Royals and Ethel Davis:

Betty Jo Royals    b. 11/13/1944          m. Mack Summerlin

| | | |
|---|---|---|
| Layton Royals | b. 1/4/1945 | m. Janie Avanell Corbitt 8/18/1972 |
| Sarah Bell Royals | b. 3/3/1947 | m. Marvin Morgan 6/3/1967 |

Clayton Royals died March 29, 1992 in Ware County, Ga. He is buried in the Kettle Creek Church Cemetery in Ware County, Ga.

Betty Jo Royals, born November 13, 1944, is the daughter of Clayton Royals and Ethel Davis. She married Mack Summerlin on August 12, 1962 in Atkinson County, Ga. His parents were Allen Summerlin and Alma Bowen. Mack Summerlin was born December 19, 1935.

The children of Betty Jo Royals and Mack Summerlin:

| | | |
|---|---|---|
| Sheila Summerlin | b. 11/9/1963 | m. Donald McGee |
| Janice Summerlin | b. 10/22/1964 | m. (1) _____ |
| | | (2) Steven Powell |
| Mack O'Neal Summerlin | b. 6/3/1968 | |
| Joyce Summerlin | b. 6/3/1971 | |
| Cheryl Summerlin | b. 8/17/1976 | |

Sheila Summerlin, born November 9, 1963, is the daughter of Mack Summerlin and Betty Jo Royals. She married Donald McGee on June 4, 1988. He was born June 16, 1957 and is the son of W. D. McGee and Carolyn Murphy.

Their child:

| | |
|---|---|
| David McGee | b. 2/17/1989 |

Janice Summerlin, born October 22, 1964, is the daughter of Mack Summerlin and Betty Jo Royals. Her second marriage is to Steven Powell. They married on June 12, 1986. Steve is the son of William Powell and Mary Sutton.

The child of Janice Summerlin and Steven Powell:

| | |
|---|---|
| Dustin Powell | b. 4/9/1989 |

Clarence Royals, born March 14, 1911, was the son of Joel Wilson Ryals and Bessie Royals. He married Eileen Ricketson on March 31, 1944.

Their child:

Clyde Wayne Royals     b. 1953                    m. Edna Robbin Steedley

Clarence Royals died May 7, 1989 and is buried at Sweetwater Cemetery. He has no other descendants as his son has no children.

Wilson Royals, born June 18, 1913  died July 5, 1981, was the son of Joel Wilson Ryals and Bessie Royals. He married Audice Wright on October 16, 1932 in Coffee County, Ga.

Their children:

Willameana Royals
Joelene Royals

Annie Belle Royals, born July 18, 1909  died October 24, 1943, was the daughter of Joel Wilson Ryals and Bessie Royals. She was married two times, (1) J. C.Sweat on February 26, 1927 in Coffee, Ga., and (2) Benefield. It is not known which husband is the father of the children. She is buried at the Old Royals Church better known as Wesley Chapel Holiness Baptist Church.

The children of Annie Belle Royals:

Leo
Clyde

Elton Royals, born August 29, 1925 in Coffee County, Ga., died September 30, 1992, was the son of Joel Wilson Ryals and Bessie Royals. He married Mary Nell Silas on December 8, 1950.

38

The children of Elton Royals and Mary Nell Silas:

| | |
|---|---|
| Patricia Royals | m. _____ Anderson |
| Larry Royals | |
| Kay Royals | m. _____ Gillard |
| Dewayne Royals | |
| Shirley Jean Royals | m. _____ Youngblood |
| Linda Royals | m. _____ Lindsey |
| Marsha Royals | m. _____ Mizell |

Joel William Royals, born April 24, 1921, was the son of Joel Wilson Ryals and Bessie Royals. He married Alma Morgan on March 15, 1945.

The children of Joel William Royals and Alma Morgan:

| | | |
|---|---|---|
| Christine Royals | b. 9/6/1944 | m. _____ Lott |
| Johnny Royals | | |
| Peggy Royals | | m. _____ Taylor |
| Rosa Royals | | m. _____ Williams |

William Royals died April 14, 1994.

Irene Ryals, born December 7, 1879 in Dodge County, Ga., was the daughter of John Calvin Ryals and Roxie Rebecca Coleman. She married Elias Metts on December 21, 1899. Elias Metts, born December 18, 1872, was the son of Micajah Metts and Ellender Rowe.

The children of Irene Ryals and Elias Metts:

| | | | |
|---|---|---|---|
| Aaron Metts | b. 12/31/1900 | d. 8/28/1901 | |
| Dan Metts | b. 12/27/1905 | d. 9/21/1961 | m. Ollie Mae Guess |
| Elton Metts | b. 4/2/1911 | d. 11/26/1970 | m. Vera Morris |
| William Metts | b. 6/5/1903 | d. 10/6/1991 | m. Janie _____ |
| Henry Metts | b. 8/5/1909 | d. 5/11/1979 | m. Rebecca Merritt |
| Beulah Metts | b. 7/14/1918 | | m. James D. Carver |
| Blannie Metts | b. 9/6/1920 | | m. Edison Henry Youngblood |

Elias Metts died in Coffee County, Ga. on January 24, 1958. Irene Ryals died in Coffee County, Ga. on December 27, 1975. They are both buried at Wesley Chapel.

Beulah Metts, born July 14, 1918 in Atkinson County, Ga., is the daughter of Irene Ryals and Elias Metts. She married James D. Carver on September 1, 1934 in Atkinson County, Ga. James D. Carver was born September 20, 1916 in Coffee County, Ga. He was the son of Allen Carver and Maude Harrell. James D. Carver was an Elder in the Primitive Baptist Association.

The children of Beulah Metts and James D. Carver:

| | | | |
|---|---|---|---|
| Rachel Carver | b. 8/6/1937 | m. (1) _____ Hamilton | |
| | | (2) Jerry Day | |
| Jimmie Sue Carver | b. 3/4/1949 | m. Noah Mancil, Jr. | |

James D. Carver died January 30, 1988 in Coffee County, Ga. and is buried at Wesley Chapel Holiness Baptist Church Cemetery.

Jimmie Sue Carver, born March 4, 1949, is the daughter of Beulah Metts and James D. Carver. She married Noah Mancil, Jr. on January 9, 1968 in Coffee County, Ga. Noah's father is Noah Mancil, Sr.

Their children:

Shannon Mancil        b. 5/13/1976
Breana Mancil         b. 4/25/1978
Mark Mancil

Rachel Carver, born August 6, 1937 in Coffee County, Ga., is the daughter of Beulah Metts and James D. Carver. She married _____ Hamilton.

Their children:

Ronald Hamilton       b. 3/13/1959
Donald Hamilton       b. 3/13/1959

Rachel Carver married Jerry Day on July, 1988. It is not know if they have any children.

Dan Metts, born December 27,1905, was the son of Irene Ryals and Elias Metts. He married Ollie Mae Guess on May 23, 1944 in Atkinson County, Ga. Ollie Mae was born August 7, 1920.

The children of Dan Metts and Ollie Mae Guess:

Roger Wayne Metts    b. 8/13/1946      m. Carolene Kite
Roy Earl Metts      b. 1/31/1950      m. Christine Dukes

Roger Wayne Metts, born August 13, 1946 in Coffee County, Ga., is the son of Dan Metts and Ollie Mae Guess. He married Carolene Kite.

Their children:

Roger Wayne Metts, Jr.
Amanda Metts

Roy Earl Metts, born January 31, 1950 in Coffee County, Ga., is the son of Dan Metts and Ollie Mae Guess. He married Christine Dukes. She had a previous marriage to a Ricketson. Roy Earl Metts and wife, Christine Dukes Ricketson Metts have no children.

Dan Metts died September 21, 1961 and is buried at Refuge Primitive Baptist Church Cemetery in Pearson, Ga.

Elton Metts, born April 2, 1911 in Coffee County, Ga., was the son of Irene Ryals and Elias Metts. He married Vera Morris. Vera was born March 27, 1911.

The children of Elton Metts and Vera Morris:

Carswell Metts     b. 3/17/1934      m. Josephine _____
Johnny Metts                    m. Lois _____
Eston Metts                       m. Carol _____

Donnie Metts
Geneva Metts        b. 11/30/1932              m. Austin McDonald
Myrtle Metts        b. 11/25/1937              m. Herbert Blitch
Margie Metts        b. 5/4/1948    d. 8//12/1972 Never married
Lucy Metts

Elton Metts died November 26, 1970 and Vera Morris Metts died May 22, 1992. They
are buried at Wesley Chapel Cemetery. Their daughter, Margie, is also buried at Wesley
Chapel Cemetery.

Carswell Metts, born March 17, 1934, was the son of Elton Metts and Vera Morris. He
married Josephine, maiden name unknown.

Their children:

Robert Metts    b. 1/9/1960    d. 1/9/1960    buried at Wesley Chapel Cemetery

Blannie Metts, born September 6, 1920, is the daughter of Irene Ryals and Elias Metts.
She married Edison Henry Youngblood. Edison Henry Youngblood, born December 7,
1920, was the son of Joe Youngblood and Rilda Geiger.

Their children:

Donalson Youngblood    b. 1/23/1949    d. 1/23/1949
Edwin Youngblood

Edison Henry Youngblood died March 24, 1991 and is buried at Wesley Chapel. His son,
Donalson Youngblood is also buried at Wesley Chapel.

William Metts, born June 5, 1903, was the son of Irene Ryals and Elias Metts. He married
Janie (maiden name not known). It is not know if there were any children. None survived
him. William Metts died October 6, 1991 in Clinch County, Ga. He is buried in the Arna
Cemetery in Atkinson County, Ga.

Hattie (Hariett) Ryals, born March 27, 1892, was the daughter of John Calvin Ryals and Roxie Ann Rebecca Coleman. She married Wiley Ellis in Coffee County, Ga. on June 30, 1906.

The child of Hattie (Harriett) Ryals and Wiley Ellis:

Clarence Ellis      b. 1907      d. 1922

Wiley Ellis died before 1907 because Hattie is found in the 1910 Coffee County Census married to Wiley Hutcheson and they have Clarence as a three year old stepson of Wiley Hutcheson. Hattie Ryals Ellis married Wyley A. Hutcheson on January 21, 1907. Wyley was born June 2, 1884 in Emanuel County, Ga. He was the son of William Bryant Hutcheson and Sallie Lawrence.

Their children:

| | | |
|---|---|---|
| Valeree Hutcheson | b. 9/7/1914 | m. Alvin (Bigun) Hulsey |
| Effie Hutcheson | b. 10/1910 | m. M. L. Chaney |
| Arlie Helen Hutcheson | b. 3/4/1917   d. 9/23/1990 | m. (1) _____ Wooten |
| | | (2) Ernest Register |
| Amy Hutcheson | b. 3/29/1920 | m. W. Ottis Lee |
| Culas W. Hutcheson | b. 8/1928 | m. Johanna H. Dietzel |

Hattie (Harriett) Ryals died January 18, 1976. She is buried in the Douglas City Cemetery. Wiley A. Hutcheson married again at the age of 95 to Lola Mae Waller. He then died October 27, 1980 and was buried in the Douglas City Cemetery.

Valeree Hutcheson, born September 7, 1914, was the daughter of Hattie (Harriett) Ryals and Wiley A. Hutcheson. She married Alvin (Bigun) Hulsey. They had no children.

Effie Hutcheson, born October, 1910, was the daughter of Hattie (Harriett) Ryals and Wiley A. Hutcheson. She married M. L. Chaney.

The children of Effie Hutcheson and M. L. Chaney:

Bob Chaney
Billy Chaney
Dixie Chaney

Arlie Helen Hutcheson, born March 4, 1917 in Coffee County, Ga., was the daughter of Hattie (Harriett) Ryals and Wiley A. Hutcheson. She married _____ Wooten.

Their child:

Ty Wooten        b.                    m. Nell Chaney

Arlie Helen Hutcheson married the second time to Ernest Register. Ernest Register preceeded his wife in death. The date is not known. Arlie Helen Hutcheson Register died September 23, 1990 in Tift County, Ga. She is buried in the Douglas City Cemetery.

Ty Wooten is the son of Arlie Helen Hutcheson and Ernest Register. He married Nell Chaney. Nell Chaney was born March 21, 1941.

Their child:

James Alvin Wooten    b. 10/14/1965

Amy Hutcheson, born March 29, 1920, was the daughter of Hattie (Harriett) Ryals and Wyley A. Hutcheson. She married W. Ottis Lee.

The children of Amy Hutcheson and W. Ottis Lee:

Wayne Lee
Amy Ann Lee
Brenda Joy Lee

Culas W. Hutcheson, born August, 1928, is the son of Hattie (Harriett) Ryals and Wyley A. Hutcheson. He married Johanna Hildegarde Dietzel on July 6, 1954.

Their children:

Culas W. (Mike) Hutcheson, Jr.
Mark Hutcheson
Lynn Hutcheson
Heidi Hutcheson

# THE ADAMS FAMILY

William Riley Adams was the son of Ezekiel Willoughby Adams. His mother is not known. He was born 1802 in S.C. and died 1890 in Bradford County, Fla. He married Sarah Fletcher. She was born 1805 in Bullock County, Ga. Her parents were Joseph Fletcher, Sr. and Elizabeth Lanier.

Their children:

| | | |
|---|---|---|
| Ezekiel Adams | b. 1825 | m. Martha _____ |
| Willoughby Adams | b. 1828 | m. Ann Harrell |
| John Q. Adams | b. 1830 | |
| David Adams | b. 1834 | |
| Mary Adams | b. 1840 | (Never married but had several children) |
| Delilah Adams | b. 1843 | m. William R. Wright |
| Jemima Jane Adams | b. 1843 | m. Eli Ricketson |
| Elizabeth Adams | b. 1824 | m. William Hurst |
| Joseph Adams | b. 1847 | m. Annie Davis |
| Lucinda Adams | b. 1838 | m. Benajah Kirkland |
| Martha Adams | b. | |
| Amos Adams | b. 1835 | m. Amanda Davis |
| William Riley Adams, Jr. | b. 1850 | m. Annie Lott |

(Delilah and Jemima were twins.)

Willoughby Adams was born November 27, 1828 in Appling County, Ga. He was the son of William Ryley Adams and Sarah Fletcher. He married Ann Harrell in 1857. She was born in 1834 and was the daughter of Lovett Harrell and Susan (Susanna) Nipper.

Their children:

| | | | |
|---|---|---|---|
| Susan Adams | b. 1860 | d. 6/2/1924 | m. Allen Joiner |
| Sarah Adams | b. 1862 | | m. Seaborn Fales |
| William R. Adams | b. 1863 | d. 3/1890 | Never married |
| Lovett (Love) Adams | b. 5/6/1865 | d. 9/16/1935 | m. Della Harrell |

| William B. Adams | b. 2/13/1866 d. 4/6/1947 | m. (1) Mamie Dell War |
| | | (2) Mary Tanner |
| Perry Adams | b. 1869 | d. 11/21/1936 m. Linnie McLeod |
| Bryant Adams | b. 1871 | m. Temperance Ellis |
| Elizabeth (Betty) Adams | b. 1873 | m. James (Jim) Spivey |

Willoughby Adams enlisted September 1862 in Co. "K", 63rd Georgia Volunteer Infantry Regiment and served until the end of the war. He was home on sick leave when the war ended. He was granted a Confederate pension in 1910. He died November 2, 1910. Ann Harrell Adams died February 22, 1915. They are both buried in the Harrell Grove Cemetery in Coffee County, Ga. Their farm was in Coffee County until Atkinson County was formed. It was located in Atkinson County after 1918.

Elizabeth Adams, born 1824, was the daughter of William Riley Adams and Sarah Fletcher. She married William Hurst.

Their children:

| Lawrence Hurst | b. 1844 | Never married |
| Aaron Hurst | b. 1846 | m. Martha Tyson |
| Jane Hurst | b. 1848 | m. James Champion |
| William R. Hurst | b. 1850 | m. (1) Pinkie Harrell |
| | | (2) Annie Lott |
| Mary Ann Hurst | b. | m. Josh Hightower |

# THE CADWELL FAMILY

The first records of the Cadwell family was in Hartford, Connecticut in 1652. Thomas Cadwell located in Hartford, Conn. in 1652. He married in 1658 to Elizabeth Stebbins, the daughter of Deacon Edward Stebbins. Elizabeth was the widow of Robert Wilson.

Their children:

| | | |
|---|---|---|
| Mary Cadwell | b. 1/8/1659 | m. _____Dickens |
| Edward Cadwell | b. 11/1/1660 | |
| Thomas Cadwell | b. 12/5/1662 | m. Hannah Butler |
| Edw. Cadwell | b. 7/14/1664 | |
| Matthew Cadwell | b. 10/5/1668 | |
| Abigail Cadwell | b. 11/26/1670 | |
| Elizabeth Cadwell | b. 12/1/1672 | |
| Samuel Cadwell | b. 4/20/1675 | |
| Hannah Cadwell | b. 8/22/1677 | |
| Melhit-a'bell Cadwell | b. 1/12/1679 | |

Thomas Cadwell died October 9, 1694.

Thomas Cadwell, b. December 5, 1662, was the son of Thomas Cadwell and Elizabeth Stebbins. He married Hannah Butler on September 23, 1687.

Their children:

| | | |
|---|---|---|
| Thomas Cadwell | b. 6/30/1689 | |
| Jonath Cadwell | b. 8/15/1694 | |
| James Cadwell | b. 4/3/1697 | m. Sarah Merry |
| Hanna Cadwell | b. 4/8/1699 | |
| Moses Cadwell | b. 7/7/1703 | |
| Louis Cadwell | b. 2/18/1705-06 | |
| Aaron Cadwell | b. 4/9/1710 | |

Moses Cadwell, born July 7, 1703, was the son of Thomas Cadwell and wife Hannah Butler.

He had the following children:

Lois Penelope, Jonathan, Lois, Timothy, Olie, Timothy. All died young except for Penelope and Jonathan.

James Cadwell, born April 3, 1697 and died August 29, 1771, was the son of Thomas Cadwell and Hannah Butler. He married Sarah Merry on July 24, 1734.

Their Children:

| | | |
|---|---|---|
| Christian Cadwell | b. 9/24/1735 | |
| Sarah Cadwell | b. 8/6/1737 | |
| Peletiah Cadwell | b. 12/2/1739 | |
| James Cadwell | b. 12/26/1742 | m. Mary Foot |

James Cadwell, born December 26, 1742, was the son of James Cadwell and Sarah Merry. He married Mary Foot on November 19, 1767.

Their children:

| | |
|---|---|
| Aaron Cadwell | baptized 11/6/1768 |
| Mary Cadwell | baptized 11/11/1770 |
| Rhoda Cadwell | baptized 2/7/1773 |
| James Cadwell | baptized 7/30/1775 |
| Martin Cadwell | baptized 2/15/1778 |
| Allyn (Allen) Cadwell | born around 1780 |

Allyn (Allen) Cadwell, born around 1780, was the son of James Cadwell and Mary Foot. He came to Wilkinson County, Georgia with his brother, Martin. He married a _____ Colley (Cowey or Cauley) who probably died when her daughter, Charlotte, was born. Allyn possibly had 2 wives because indications show that _____ Colley had one daughter.

49

Children of Allyn (Allen) Cadwell:

| | |
|---|---|
| Margaret (Marge) Cadwell | m. Benjamin Hamilton |
| Rebecca Cadwell | m. Abel Wright |
| Charlotte Cadwell    b. 1811 Wilkinson Co., Ga. d. 1894-98 | |
| | m. Reuben Flournoy Burch I |

# THE CARVER FAMILY

Needham Carver, born February 8, 1866, was the son of Joseph Carver and Polly Purvis.
He married Amanda Thomas. Amanda Thomas was born August 31, 1866.

Their children:

Tom Carver
Lawton Carver b. 6/3/1911   d. 9/11/1958  m. Pearl  b. 1/21/1913 d. 9/12/1991
(Both are buried at Vickers Cemetery)
James Carver  b. 8/18/1900  d. 12/10/1976 m. Ola Mae   b. 11/10/1910
(Both are buried at Vickers Cemetery)
Walter Carver b. 7/28/1905  d. 11/12/1980
(Buried at Vickers Cemetery)

Polly Carver    b. 1886          m. Thomas Joiner
Mahala Carver                    m. _____ Smith
Lithie Carver                    m. _____ Joiner
Fannie Carver                    m. _____ Buchanan
Alvin Carver

Amanda Thomas Carver died September 7, 1934.  Needham Carver died December 4,
1938.  They are both buried in The Vickers Rural Cemetery in Coffee County, Ga.

(The family of Polly Carver and Thomas Joiner is listed in the Joiner Family section.)

# THE CLARKE/CLARK FAMILY

General Elijah Clarke was born in Edgecombe County, North Carolina, in 1736, the son of William Clark and wife, Mary. His brothers and sisters were Sarah Clark, Michael Clark, and John Clark. He died in Georgia, December 15, 1799. Gen. Clark married in North Carolina in 1760 to Hannah Arrington. She was born 1737 and died in 1827. Gen. Clark lived after 1774 in Wilkes County, Ga. Both of them are buried at the home plantation in Lincoln County, Ga..

Gen. Clark was granted a lot of land in the State of Georgia, of which included 2955 acres in Washington County, Ga. It was later formed into Montgomery County. Gen. Clark was a General in the Revolutionary War.

General Clark's children:

(1) John Clark, born in North Carolina in 1776, died in Florida, October 15, 1832. He married Nancy Williamson. (He was elected governor of Georgia in 1819, again in 1821. He moved to Florida in 1827.

(2) Gibson Clark, born 1772, died in 1820. He married Susanna Clark, and moved to Mississippi. He graduated in 1804, at Franklin College, which is not the University of Georgia. He was living in Telfair County, Ga., when he represented the county in the Legislature.

| | |
|---|---|
| (3) Elijah Clark, Jr. | m. Margaret Long |
| (4) Nancy Clark | m. Jesse Thompson |
| (5) Elizabeth Clark | m. Benajah Smith |
| (6) Polly Clark | m. Col. Charles Williamson |
| (7) Frances Clark | m. Edward Mounger |
| (8) Susan Clark (died young) | |

Records show that John was a General, and Elijah Jr. and Gibson were lawyers.

Elijah Clark, Jr., son of Gen. Elijah Clark, married Margaret Long. Her parents were Evans Long and Lucy Apperson.

Their children:

| | | |
|---|---|---|
| Nimrod Clark | b. 1816 in Ga. | m. Margaret |
| Charlotte Clark | b. 1810 | m. William R. Ryals |

Nimrod Clark, born 1816 in Ga., was the son of Gen. Elijah Clark and Margaret Long. He is shown in the 1850 Montgomery County, Ga. Census.

His children:

| | | |
|---|---|---|
| Joseph Clark | b. 1839 in Ga. | |
| Patrick Clark | b. 1841 in Ga. | m. Emeline M. Browning |
| William Clark | b. 1843 in Ga. | |
| Sharlotte Clark | b. 1846 in Ga. | m. Green H. Browning |
| Oran Clark | b. 1848 in Ga. | |
| Nimrod Clark | b. 1849 in Ga. | |
| John P. Clark | | m. Missouri F. Browning |

Patrick H. Clark, born 1841, married in Montgomery County, Ga. on October 8, 1863, to Emeline M. Browning. Sharlotte (Charlotte) Clark, born 1846 in Ga., married in Montgomery County, Ga. on October 15, 1868, to Green H. Browning. John P. Clark, who married in Montgomery County, Ga., November 5, 1868, to Missouri F. Browning, may have been son of Nimrod. He was born after the census was taken.

Charlotte Clark, born 1810 and died after 1870, was the daughter of Elijah Clark, Jr. and his wife Margaret Long. She was the second wife of William R. Ryals. They married in 1832. (See the family of Charlotte Clark and William R. Ryals in the Ryals Family section.)

# THE COLEMAN FAMILY

William Andrew Coleman was born in Georgia about 1826. According to the 1850 Laurens County, Ga. Census, he was living in Laurens County and was 23 years of age. His parents were Lee or Levi Coleman and wife, _____. He married around 1846 to Priscilla Wright. She was born around 1828 or 1829 in Laurens County, Ga. and was the daughter of Abel Wright and Rebecca Cadwell.

A William A. Coleman was found as a White among the Cherokee Indians in 1830. The records show that he owns but little. It is possible that this is a relative of our William Andrew Coleman. He had a wife and three children. Since William Andrew Coleman would have been about 3 at this time, this could be his father. This would explain why everyone in our family kept saying there were Cherokee Indians in our past. If this is true, then William A. Coleman could have been half Cherokee Indian with his mother as full-blooded Cherokee Indian.

William Andrew Coleman and his wife Priscilla Wright lived in Laurens County, Ga. and had the following children:

| | | |
|---|---|---|
| Sabra (Sarah) Caroline Coleman | b. about 1847 | m. Alfred T. Coleman |
| William C. Coleman | b. about 1852 | m. Mary Coleman |
| Roxie Rebecca Coleman | b. 2/24/1855 | m. John Calvin Ryals |
| Mary Eliza Coleman | b. | m. Joseph H. Evans |
| Nancy Jane Coleman | b. | Never married |
| Wade Hampton Coleman | b. about 1859 | m. (1) Emma V. Thompson |
| | | (2) Sudie Gertrude Walker |
| James Andrew Coleman | b. after 1850 | m. Christian Burch |
| General Robert Lee Coleman | b. | m. Nancy Ann Evans |
| Bartemus T. Coleman | b. | m. Mary Catherine Taylor |
| Martha J. Coleman | b. | m. Dock Sanderson |
| Joel Franklin Coleman | b. 1870 | m. Nancy Ann Rogers |

Roxie Rebecca Coleman, born February 24, 1855, died March, 1908, was the daughter of William Andrew Coleman and Priscilla Wright. She married John Calvin Ryals on August 22, 1875. They moved to Coffee County, Ga. where they had a large family. (This family is listed in the Ryals Family Section.)

James Andrew Coleman (called Andy) was born after 1850 in Laurens County, Ga. He was the son of William Andrew Coleman and Priscilla Wright. He married Christian Burch in November of 1880. Christian Burch was born October 4, 1858. She was the daughter of Charles Burch and Rebecca Yawn.

Their children:

| | | | |
|---|---|---|---|
| Anna Coleman | b. 9/1881 | d. 5/2/1886 | |
| Wade Hampton Coleman | b. 10/3/1883 | | m. (1) Mollie Clark |
| | | | (2) Nannie Elizabeth Kirkland |
| Georgia Belle Coleman | b. 1885 | | m. Cecil Hightower |
| Sadie Coleman | b. | | m. James Jones |
| Charles (Charlie) Andrew Coleman | b. 8/1/1888 | | m. Ether Wright |
| Levi Samuel Coleman | b. 6/7/1893 | | m. (1) Mollie Kirkland |
| | | | (2) Marie Morrison |
| Docia Coleman | b. 7/18/1896 | | m. Ennis Bland |
| Agnes Coleman | b. about 1898 | | m. Willie Neal Sikes |
| Hattie Coleman | Died at 4 or 5 years old | | |

The Rev. Wade Hampton Coleman (called Wade) was born in Laurens County, Ga. and died at his home in Eastman, Ga., Dodge County, about 1935. He was 76 years old. He was the son of William Andrew Coleman and Priscilla Wright. They are buried at the Coleman Cemetery near Plainfield, Dodge County, Ga. Wade Hampton Coleman was a Baptist preacher. He married first to Emma Virginia Thompson in Dodge County, Ga. on September 4, 1881. She was born in 1866 and died in August 1925. She was the daughter of Rev. John Thompson who was a pioneer Baptist minister. (Other children of Rev. John Thompson included: a daughter who married R. W. Southerland; a daughter who married Hughy Giddens; and a daughter Fannie who married an Evans.)

The Rev. Wade Coleman and his first wife lived in Dodge County, Ga. and had the following children:

| | | |
|---|---|---|
| John Andrew Coleman | b. 1882 | m. Pearl Graham |
| William Thomas Coleman | b. 9/2/1887 | m. Sallie Loveless |
| General Lee Coleman | b. 12/12/1889 | m. Emma Eunice Perry |

| | | |
|---|---|---|
| Walter Jackson Coleman | b. 1891 | m. (1) Betty Gordon |
| | | (2) Mary Coleman |
| | | (3) Annie _____ |
| Arthur Coleman | died when 12 yrs. of age | |
| Dr. Warren Ashley Coleman | b. 1895 | d. after 1937 m. Christine Edwards |
| Wade Hampton Coleman, Jr. | b. | m. Oppie Lee Peacock |
| Henry Clay Coleman | b. | m. Pauline Graham |

Joel Franklin Coleman (called Joel) was born in 1870 and died July 1935. He was the son of William Andrew Coleman and Priscilla Wright. Joel married February 9, 1890 in Dodge County, Ga. to Nancy Ann Rogers. She was born September 1873 and was the daughter of Thomas Morgan Rogers. Joel Franklin and his wife Nancy lived near Eastman, Ga. and had the following children:

| | | |
|---|---|---|
| Priscilla Coleman | b. 1890 | m. (1) Clarence McLeod |
| | | (2) Elisha Coleman |
| Nannie Coleman | b. 1892 | m. (1) Roger Smith |
| | | (2) A. Leon Mozo |
| Thomas Andrew Coleman | b. | m. (1) Laura Livingston |
| | | (2) Sybyl Couey |
| Joel Vernon Coleman | b. 4/18/1900 | m. Ann Lee |
| Clara Coleman | | m. Theo Gay |
| Arthur Coleman | | Never married |
| Oeida Coleman | | m. Tom Haislip |
| Kenneth Coleman | | |

Bartemus T. Coleman was born in Laurens County, Ga. in 1863. He died June 30, 1934. He was the son of William Andrew Coleman and Priscilla Wright. He married Mary Catherine Taylor in Dodge County, Ga. on October 14, 1880. Mary Catherine Taylor was the daughter of William Taylor and Rosa Yawn. Bartemus T. Coleman and his wife lived in Dodge County, Ga. and had the following children:

| | | |
|---|---|---|
| Samantha Priscilla Coleman | | m. Love Livingston |
| Mary Louisa Coleman | | m. Wesley Mullis |
| General Lee Coleman | (died in infancy) | |

| | | |
|---|---|---|
| William Levi Coleman | | m. Dora Darsey |
| Wade Andy Coleman | b. 12/15/1888 | m. Ida Rogers |
| Nancy Rosella Coleman | b. 8/8/1890 | m. Willie Freeman Bracewell |
| Martha Caroline Coleman | b. 1/5/1892 | m. Iverson Comer Fordham |
| Isaac Coleman | (Died at 16 years) | |
| Elvenia Coleman | | m. Cecil Moore |
| Lugenia Coleman | | m. Willie Floyd |
| Sarah Lucretia Coleman | | m. Lige Carr |
| Mamie Ethel Coleman | b. 1900 | Never married |
| Zuma Coleman | b. 1902 | Never married |
| Zuna Coleman | b. 1902 d. 1904 | |

Elvenia and Lugenia Colman were twins. Zuma and Zuna Coleman were twins.

# THE EASON FAMILY

William Eason died in Nash County, N. C., March 1, 1783. He will named his three sons as:

Samuel Eason
Dempsey Eason
John Eason

Samuel Eason was the son of William Eason. He married Edith. He died December 3, 1800 in Nash County, N. C. He named his children in his will. The daughters that were married were named by their last name.

| | |
|---|---|
| William Eason | |
| Isaias Eason | |
| Edith Eason | m. Strickland |
| Eunice Eason | m. Strickland |
| Mary Eason | m. Strickland |
| Elizabeth Eason | m. Keith |
| Milley Eason | m. Jacob Joiner |
| Ruth Eason | |

# THE HARRELL FAMILY

Francis Harrell was living in Nansemond County, Virginia in 1731. He sold 50 acres of land to William Baker and moved to Bertie County, North Carolina by 1734. His will was recorded there in 1759.

Jacob Harrell (son of Francis Harrell) may have first moved to Anson County, North Carolina (for his son, Levi, was said to have been born there). Jacob Harrell was later in Craven County South Carolina, where he received nearly 1,000 acres of land between 1768 and 1773. Jacob Harrell's will of January 22, 1787 mentioned his wife, but not her name.

His children:

Levi
Jasper
Lewis

Levi Harrell (son of Jacob Harrell) was born in Anson County, N. C. in 1750. He served in the Revolutionary War in South Carolina, under Gen. Francis Marion. He died after the 1790 census in Orangeburg County, South Carolina. He married 1st in 1776 to a Mrs. Cole of Irish descent (family tradition). (It is also family tradition that the Harrell family came to the United States from Ireland.)

Their Children:

| | | | |
|---|---|---|---|
| Asa Harrell | b. 1787 | d. 1850 | m. Elizabeth Keen |
| Levi Harrell | b. 9/16/1777 | d. 12/21/1865 | m. Elizabeth Holt |
| Frances Harrell | b. 1781 | d. 1841 | m. Elizabeth (Betsy) Owens |
| William I. Harrell | b. 1784 | d. 5/23/1866 | m. Catherine Bass |

Levi Harrell (son of Jacob Harrell) married the second time to Esther White. They had the following children:

| | |
|---|---|
| Jacob Harrell | b. 1804 |

| Ethelred Harrell | b. around 1800 | m. Polly Thompson |
| Samuel Harrell | b. | m. Elizabeth Jones |
| Lovett Harrell | b. about 1800 | m. Susan Nipper |
| Esther Harrell | b. 12/13/1801 | m. Isaac Allen |

Levi Harrell (son of Jacob Harrell) died 1806 in Orangeburg Dist., South Carolina.

Asa Harrell was the son of Levi Harrell and wife, Mrs. Cole. He was born in South Carolina in 1789. He moved to Pulaski County, Ga. and served in War of 1812 (as a private) under General David Blackshear. He married Elizabeth Keen in 1815. She was born in North Carolina and was the daughter of John Keen.

They had several children including:

Willis P. Harrell  b. 1820   d. 12/7/1864   m. Sophia Hendley

Willis P. Harrell, born in Pulaski County, Ga. in 1820, was the son of Asa Harrell and Elizabeth Keen. He served as a Lieutenant in the Confederate States Army (Civil War) and died in a military hospital in Macon, Ga. on December 7, 1864. He married Sophia Hendley in Pulaski County, Ga. on April 18, 1850. She was born March 10, 1828, in Pulaski County, Ga. and died in Dodge County, Ga. on July 10, 1910.

Their children:

| Millie Ann Harrell | |
| John James Harrell | m. Phoebe Hamilton |
| Willis P. Harrell, Jr. | m. Viola Studstill |
| Mary Jane Harrell | m. William Burt |

Lovett Harrell was born in North Carolina in 1800. He was a son of Levi Harrell (R.S.) and his first wife, Mrs. Cole. He came to Pulaski County, Ga. with his parents and was married there, October 28, 1830, to Susan Nipper. Susan Nipper was born in 1815 in Georgia.

The children of Lovett Harrell and Susan Nipper:

| | | | |
|---|---|---|---|
| Ann Harrell | b. 1834 | | m. Willoughby Adams |
| Elizabeth Harrell | b. 1837 | | m. Ivy Ricketson, died in CSA |
| William Harrell | b. 1839 | | Died single in CSA |
| Mary Harrell | b. 1841 | d. 1907 | Never married |
| Jane "Pinky" Harrell | b. 1843 | | m. Harden Joiner |
| Sarah Harrell | b. 1845 | | Never married |
| Lovett Harrell | b. 1847 | | m. Dlphia Hall |
| Susan Harrell | b. 1849 | | m. William Adams, 7/20/1879 (His second wife) |
| Priscilla "Prissy" Harrell | b. 1853 | | m. James Lankford |

Lovett Harrell moved to what is now Coffee County, Ga. after 1850. He lived there until his death, August 9, 1896. Susan Nipper Harrell died March of 1855 in Coffee County, Ga. It is not known where they are buried.

William Harrell, son of Lovett Harrell and Susan Nipper, enlisted March 4, 1862 in Company "C", 50th Georgia Regiment of the Confederate Army of Coffee County. He served just a short time and died in camp in Savannah on May 3, 1862.

Ann Harrell, daughter of Lovett Harrell and Susan Nipper, married Willoughby Adams. (See her family in the Adams Family Section.)

# THE LONG FAMILY

Samuel Long was married to Mary _____.

Their children:

| | | | |
|---|---|---|---|
| Bromfield Long | b. | d. 7/20/1778 | m. Sarah Brown |
| Mary Long | | | |
| Elizabeth Long | | | |

Bromfield Long was the son of Samuel and Mary Long.

They had the following children:

| | | | |
|---|---|---|---|
| Reuben Long | b. 1730 | d. 12/29/1791 | m. Mary Harrison |
| John Long | | | |
| Bromfield Long | | | |
| Gabriel Long | | | |
| Thomas Long | | | |
| Benjamin Long | | | |
| Nancy Long | | | |
| Betty Long | | | m. Frances Apperson |
| Milly Long | | | |

Reuben Long, born 1730 in Va., died December 29, 1791, was the son of Bromfield Long and his wife, Sarah Brown. He married, prior to 1751, to Mary Harrison. Mary Harrison was born 1732 in Virginia and died 1791. He served as a Virginia Patriot.

Their children:

| | | | |
|---|---|---|---|
| Gabriel Long | | | |
| Anderson Long | | | |
| Nicholas Long | | | |
| Nimrod Long | | | |
| Evans Long | b. 1759 | d. 1819 | m. Lucy Apperson |

Frances Long
Peggy Long
Polly Long

Evans Long was born in Culpepper County, Virginia. He died 1819 in Twiggs County, Georgia. Evans Long married Lucy Apperson before 1793. Lucy was born in Spotsylvania County, Virginia around 1762. She died after 1822.

Their children:

| | | | |
|---|---|---|---|
| Mary Long | b. 1783 | d. 1872 | m. William Crocker |
| Margaret Long | | | m. Elijah Clark, Jr. |
| Frances Long | b. 10/19/1786 | d. 10/5/1853 | m. William Hudson |
| Lunceford Long | | | m. Nancy Jackson |
| Lucinda Long | | | m. John Owens |
| Sarah Ann Long | | | m. Tuttle Moreland |
| Nimrod Washington Long | | | m. Catherine Davis |

Margaret Long was the daughter of Evans Long and Lucy Apperson. She married Elijah Clark, Jr. (See their family under the Clark Family Section.)

# THE WRIGHT FAMILY

Abel Wright was born in North Carolina in 1800, according to the Laurens County, Ga. 1850 Census. It is not known for sure who his parents are. He could have been the son of Winfield Wright, who was born in North Carolina in 1777, and his wife, Elizabeth, who was born in North Carolina in 1781. If he is the son of Winfield Wright, then he is grandson of another Winfield Wright, whose will was probated in Granville County, North Carolina, in 1783. Those mentioned were: Hannah, Susanna, Mary P., Winfield, Thomas, John, William and Benjamin.

Abel Wright, Kinson Wright, and William Wright drew land in the Lottery of 1819 and were living in Laurens County, Ga. William had two draws; Kinson had two draws; and Abel had one draw. They were probably brothers. Abel Wright named one of his sons, Kinson.

Abel Wright, born in North Carolina in 1800, was living in Laurens County, Ga. as early as 1819. He married Rebecca Cadwell on January 13, 1820, in Laurens County, Ga.

Their children:

| | | |
|---|---|---|
| Rebecca Wright (Twin) | b. about 1825 | |
| F. Kinson Wright (Twin) | b. about 1825 | m. Lucinda Coleman |
| Micajah Wright | b. about 1828 | m. (1) Susanna L. Lee |
| | | (2) Lydia Wright |
| | | (3) Caroline H. Powell |
| Priscilla Wright | b. aobut 1829 | m. William Andrew Coleman |
| Sarah Wright | b. about 1833 | m. Henry Wise (or Weeks) |
| Emily Wright | b. about 1835 | m. William J. Coleman |
| Roxianna Wright | b. about 1838 | m. William Hannibal Weeks |
| Mary Wright (Twin) | b. about 1840 | |
| Jane Wright (Twin) | b. about 1840 | |
| Wade Wright | b. about 1843 | |
| James Bartow Wright | b. 11/7/1847 | m. Samantha Nicholson |

It is not known when Abel Wright died but his wife, Rebecca Cadwell Wright was dead before 1850 Census. Their large family continued to multiply and spead out.

Priscilla Wright, born about 1829, was 21 years old at 1850 Census of Laurens County. She was the daughter of Abel Wright and Rebecca Cadwell. She married William Andrew Coleman around 1846. (See their family in the Coleman Family section.)

F. Kinson Wright, born about 1825, was a twin to Rebecca. He was the son of Abel Wright and Rebecca Cadwell. He married Lucinda Coleman on September 2, 1847 in Laurens County, Ga. They were living in Laurens County in 1850 and had two children.

William A. Wright     b. about 1848
Abel T. Wright       b. about 1849

Micajah Wright, born about 1828, was the son of Abel Wright and Rebecca Cadwell. He married Susanna L. Lee on October 29, 1849 in Pulaski County, Ga. She was the daughter of William Lee. She died before 1850. They had one child.

Sarah Wright             Never married. (She died when she was 18 years old.)

Micajah (Cagie) married Lydia Wright the second time. They had five children:

| | | |
|---|---|---|
| Mary Wright | b. about 1862 d. 1930 | m. John Powell |
| Edward Wright (Edd) | b. about 1864 | m. Nora Crumpton |
| Newton Hamilton Wright (Hamp) | b. about 1866 | m. Sybil Ann Livingston |
| Warren Wright | b. 12/7/1868 | m. Nancy Ann Coleman |
| Corine Wright | b. | m. (1) Caswell Rowland |
| | | (2) Martin Livingston |

Micajah Wright (Cagie) married the third time to Caroline H. Powell (Tiny) on August 1, 1885.

James Bartow Wright, born November 7, 1847, in Laurens County and died in Dodge County on August 4, 1926. He was the son of Abel Wright and Rebecca Cadwell. He married Samantha Ann Frances Nicholson on June 1, 1866 in Pulaski County, Ga. She was born September 5, 1849 and died September 4, 1929. They lived in Dodge County.

The children of James Bartow Wright and Samantha Ann Frances Nicholson:

| | | | |
|---|---|---|---|
| Samuel Dorsey Wright | b. 10/18/1867 | | |
| James Dalton Wright | b. | d. 1/21/1944 | m. Drucilla Livingston |
| John Ashley Wright | b. 2/12/1871 | | m. Emma Moore |
| Amanda Idelia Wright | b. 1/14/1873 | | m. John Champion |
| Lawrence Clark Wright | b. 11/6/1874 | d. 3/4/1942 | Never married |
| Daniel Ross Wright | b. 11/4/1876 | | m. Carrie Tuggle |
| William Preston Wright | b. 8/3/1879 | | m. Etta Mullis |
| Jackson Nathaniel Wright | b. 4/6/1881 | d. before 1945 | Never married |
| Estelle Columbia Wright | b. 7/26/1883 | | m. John Crowell |
| Minnie Ann Serenie Wright | b. 4/6/1887 | | m. Henry Livingston |
| Odie May Wright | b. 10/10/1891 | d. 1/20/1911 | m. Thomas Graham |
| Claude Washington Wright | b. 11/24/1895 | | m. Vienna Jane Brown |

# DESCENDANTS OF WILLIAM JOINER AND SABREY RYALS

The family of William and Sabrey Ryals Joiner meet every year on the first Sunday in July for a family reunion. They met for about the 40th time in July of 1993. There were about 100 family members that attended. They brought lunch and enjoyed a wonderful dinner and fellowship. It is held each year in Willacoochee, Ga. at the Willacoochee Holiness Baptist Church.

Some old pictures have been found and a family photo album was started. We're hoping to hold onto some memories in this fast world and preserve our family history with this book.

William Joiner and Sabrey Ryals were married August 23, 1900 in Coffee County, Ga. William's parents were Allen Joiner and Susan Adams. Sabrey's parents were John Calvin Ryals and Roxie Coleman. The Joiner and Ryals ancestors came from England.

William and Sabrey Joiner had 10 children: Mose Joiner, Willie Lee Joiner, Arthur Joiner, Olif Joiner, Ben Agie Joiner, Elie Joiner, Bithie Joiner, Jeff Joiner, Roscoe Joiner, and Annie Belle Joiner. Bithie, Jeff, and Arthur are the only children living at this time. There are grandchildren and great-grandchildren, etc., to carry on the tradition of dinner together in July.

The first birthday dinner was held outside Willacoochee, Ga. at the home of Jeff Joiner in 1954. The place was changed from time to time and has finally settled at the Willacoochee Holiness Baptist Church. It was originally a birthday dinner for Grandma Sabrey Joiner since her birthday was on July 9. She died August 17, 1974 and we skipped at least one year after her death. We decided to carry on the tradition as a Joiner Reunion.

# THE MOSE JOINER FAMILY

Mose Joiner, born July 7, 1901, was the son of William Joiner and Sabrey Carolina Ryals. He married Nellie Victoria Todd on September 19, 1920 in Coffee County, Ga. Nellie was born July 12, 1904 and was the daughter of John N. Todd and Ella Spivey.

Their children:

| | | | |
|---|---|---|---|
| John William Joiner | b. 12/14/1921 | | m. Ernie Maudeen Bookout |
| Spencer Lee Joiner | b. 7/31/1924 | | m. Eleanor D. (Doodle) Hattaway |
| Ivey Warren Joiner | b. 5/9/1926 | d. 1991 | m. (1) Thelma Joyce Yarbrough |
| | | | (2) Doris Wolfanger |
| Robert Joiner | b. 10/9/1925 | | |

Mose Joiner died January 23, 1935 of pneumonia. He is buried at Mt. Union Holiness Baptist (Lax) Church Cemetery. Nellie married again to Jim Spells. Nellie died September 6, 1983 and is buried at the Douglas City Cemetery.

John William Joiner, b. December 14, 1921 in Coffee County, Ga., is the son of Mose Joiner and Nellie Victoria Todd. He married Ernie Maudeen Bookout on June 15, 1949. They reside in Acworth, Ga.

Their children:

| | | |
|---|---|---|
| Janet Marie Joiner | b. 4/19/1951 | m. Ronnie Lee Bentley |
| Michael Joseph Joiner | b. 1/27/1954 | m. Nora Jean Thompson |

Janet Marie Joiner, born April 19, 1951, is the daughter of John William Joiner and Ernie Maudean Bookout. She married Ronnie Lee Bentley on April 4, 1970. Ronnie was born on August 3, 1949.

Their children:

| | |
|---|---|
| Anne Marie Bentley | b. 3/2/1972 |
| Rhonda Lynn Bentley | b. 9/23/1976 |
| Stephen Paul Bentley | b. 4/30/1984 |

Anne Marie Bentley, born March 2, 1972, is the daughter of Ronnie Lee Bentley and Janet Marie Joiner.

Her child:

Amanda Marie Cox     b. 9/28/1990

Michael Joseph Joiner, born January 27, 1954, is the son of John William Joiner and Ernie Maudean Bookout. He married Nora Jean Thompson on February 10, 1973.

Their children:

David William Joiner     b. 6/21/1977
Julie Michele Joiner     b. 10/13/1979

Spencer Lee Joiner, born July 31, 1924, is the son of Mose Joiner and Nellie Victoria Todd. He married Eleanor Delois (Doodle) Hattaway on November 1, 1953. She was born December 2, 1935. They reside in Douglas, Ga.

Their children:

| | | |
|---|---|---|
| Judy Delois Joiner | b. 2/17/1955 | m. Edwin Jerome Taylor |
| Debra Jean (Debbie) Joiner | b. 1/28/1957 | m. Ronald Troy Highsmith |
| Ellen Rebecca (Becky) Joiner | b. 6/28/1959 | m. Ronnie Keith Chaney |
| Peggy Lynn Joiner | b. 11/10/1961 | m. Gary Lee Johnson |
| Cathy Jo Joiner | b. 1/17/1967 | |
| Sandra Kay Joiner | b. 11/4/1964 | |

Judy Delois Joiner, born February 17, 1955, is the daughter of Spencer Lee Joiner and Eleanor Delois (Doodle) Hattaway. She married Edwin Jerome Taylor. He was born November 28, 1960.

Their children:

James Drury Taylor     b. 11/6/1981
Jeffery Jerome Taylor     b. 5/4/1984

69

Debra Jean (Debbie) Joiner, born January 28, 1957, is the daughter of Spencer Lee Joiner and Eleanor Delois (Doodle) Hattaway. She married Ronald Troy Highsmith on June 18, 1989.

Ellen Rebecca (Becky) Joiner, born June 28, 1959, is the daughter of Spencer Lee Joiner and Eleanor Delois (Doodle) Hattaway. She married Ronnie Keith Chaney on February 27, 1988. He was born on October 15, 1964.

Their children:

Ronnie Keith Chaney, Jr.    b. 5/3/1989
Landon Trent Chaney         b. 1/31/1991

Peggy Lynn Joiner, born November 10, 1961, is the daughter of Spencer Lee Joiner and Eleanor Delois (Doodle) Hattaway. She married Gary Lee Johnson on June 20, 1986. He was born on May 9, 1963.

Their children:

Cody Lee Johnson       b. 4/17/1989

Ivey Warren Joiner, born May 9, 1926, died 1991, was the son of Mose Joiner and Nellie Victoria Todd. He married Thelma Joyce Yarbrough.

Their children:

| Tommy Joiner | b. 9/13/1945 | m. Linda McLean |
| Mary Nell Joiner | | m. (1) Richard Ivens |
| | | (2) Gregory Hill |
| | | (3) Cranston Brown |
| | | (4) Cranston Brown |
| Barbara Ann Joiner | b. 2/26/1949 | m. Larry Chaney |
| Ivey Larry Joiner | b. 10/5/1952 | m. Virginia Lee Brooks |
| Darrell Joiner | b. 12/15/1954? | m. Sharon Kay Tranks |
| Charlie Joiner | b. 4/6/1959 | m. Denise |
| Glenn Joiner | b. 2/20/1961 | m. Gina |

Ivey Warren Joiner, born May 9, 1926, married the second time to Doris Wolfanger.

Tommy Joiner, born September 13, 1945, is the son of Ivey Warren Joiner and Thelma Joyce Yarbrough. He married Linda McLean on August 21, 1964.

Their children:

| Lamar Joiner | b. 12/22/1974 |
| Brad Joiner | b. 3/17/1981 |

Mary Nell Joiner is the daughter of Ivey Warren Joiner and Thelma Joyce Yarbrough. She married Richard Ivens, Gregory Hill, and Cranston Brown, the third and fourth time.

Mary Nell's children:

| Richard Warren (Ricky) Ivens | b. 9/24/1965 | | |
| Lisa Ann Joiner | b. 6/13/1968 | m. | _____ Cook |
| Gregory Webster Hill | b. 1/1/1977 | | |

Barbara Ann Joiner, born February 26, 1949, is the daughter of Ivey Warren Joiner and Thelma Joyce Yarbrough. She married Larry Chaney on August 3, 1969.

Their children:

| Duanne Chaney | b. 8/31/1974 |
| Marci Chaney | b. 8/31/1979 |

Ivey Larry Joiner, born October 5, 1952, is the son of Ivey Warren Joiner and Thelma Joyce Yarbrough. He married Virginia Lee Brooks on October 28, 1972.

Their children:

| Jennifer Michelle Joiner | b. 10/3/1974 d. 5/1979 |
| Mary Allison Joiner | b. 7/7/1982 |
| Larry Joshua Joiner | b. 9/20/1985 |
| Jason Todd Joiner | b. 8/14/1986 |

Darrell Joiner, born December 15, 1954, is the son of Ivey Warren Joiner and Thelma Joyce Yarbrough. He married Sharon Kay Tranks on December 21, 1974. Sharon was born July 29, 1956. Darrell is a Baptist Preacher.

Their children:

Christie Kay Joiner          b. 4/25/1975

Charlie Joiner, born April 6, 1959, is the son of Ivey Warren Joiner and Thelma Joyce Yarbrough. He married Denise.

Their child:

Randy Joiner

Glenn Joiner, born February 20, 1961, is the son of Ivey Warren Joiner and Thelma Joyce Yarbrough. He married Gina.

Their children:

April Joiner
Glenn Joiner, Jr.

## WILLIE LEE JOINER FAMILY

Willie Lee Joiner, born May 15, 1903, died November 26, 1986, was the son of William
Joiner and Sabrey Carolina Ryals. He married Beulah Lott on September 13, 1943 in
Coffee County, Ga. Beulah was born April 28, 1895 and died January 29, 1981. Willie
and Beulah had no children. They divorced after Beulah shot Willie's two toes off in a
misunderstanding. She then married Mackie Rowe. Willie died of a stroke and pneumonia
at Lakeland hospital and was buried in the Mt. Union Holiness Baptist (Lax) Cemetery.

## ARTHUR JOINER FAMILY

Arthur Joiner, born November 14, 1915, is the son of William Joiner and Sabrey Carolina Ryals. He married Alice McNatt on July 8, 1934. Alice was born August 14, 1918. She is the daughter of Joe Ed McNatt and Mary Emma Luke. They reside in Orlando, Fla.

Their children:

| | | | |
|---|---|---|---|
| Mary Alice Joiner | b. 7/29/1935 | m. (1) Cecil Bishop | |
| | | (2) Lewis Robert Worthy | |
| Earl (Buddy) Joiner | b. 3/28/1937 | m. Winnell (Nell) Soles | |
| James Joiner | b. 4/20/1939 | d. 6/25/1940 | |
| Shirley Joiner | b. 9/19/1941 | m. Pete Salmon | |
| Joe Gary Joiner | b. 7/17/1943 | m. Joyce Powell | |
| Dorothy Sue Joiner | b. 7/27/1945 | m. Lester Bailey | |
| Bennie David Joiner | b. 11/5/1948 | d. 11/26/1948 | |
| Arthur Joiner, Jr. | b. 5/7/1951 | m. (1) Carolyn Gibbs | |
| | | (2) Roberta Hundley | |
| George Samuel (Sammy) Joiner | b. 10/30/1955 | | |

Mary Alice Joiner, born July 29, 1935, is the daughter of Arthur Joiner and Alice McNatt. She married Cecil Bishop on January 9, 1954. Cecil was born December 22, 1922 and and they had one child:

Gail Bishop    b. 10/22/1956        m. (1) Mark Sellers
                                                  (2) Richard Kitchens

Cecil was driving a dump truck and had an accident. He died in May of 1957.

Mary Alice Joiner married Lewis Robert Worthy in 1958. Lewis Robert Worthy was born August 29, 1928.

Their children:

| | | |
|---|---|---|
| Lewis Robert Worthy, Jr. | b. 5/17/1959 | m. Rhonda Wheeler |
| Dennis Worthy | b. 1/21/1961 | m. Kim Honors |
| James Worthy | b. 6/7/1964 d. 4/25/1985 | |

Gail Bishop, born October 22, 1955, is the daughter of Cecil Bishop and Mary Alice Joiner. She married Mark Sellers on March 2, 1973. Mark was born April 2, 1955.

Their children:

| | |
|---|---|
| Amy Sellers | b. 12/23/1978 |
| Mary Sellers | b. 12/30/1975 |

Gail married the second time to Richard Kitchens on April 18, 1982. Richard was born September 3, 1947.

Lewis Robert Worthy, Jr., born May 17, 1959, is the son of Lewis Robert Worthy and Mary Alice Joiner. He married Rhonda Wheeler. Rhonda was born July 20, 1960.

Their children:

| | |
|---|---|
| Bobby Worthy | b. 3/1/1984 |
| Jennifer Worthy | b. 8/8/1988 |

Dennis Worthy, born January 21, 1961, is the son of Lewis Robert Worthy and Mary Alice Joiner. He married Kim Honors in 1988. Kim was born June 9. 1958.

Their children:

| | |
|---|---|
| Rebecca Worthy | b. 9/25/1988 |
| Sarah Mae Worthy | b. 6/25/1990 |

Earl (Buddy) Joiner, born March 28, 1937, is the son of Arthur Joiner and Alice McNatt. He married Winnell Soles December 6, 1957. Winnell (Nell) was born October 6, 1938. She is the daughter of Noley Soles and Lenn Carver.

Their children:

| | | |
|---|---|---|
| Lawanda Joiner | b. 3/5/1959 | m. (1) William Roger Kitts |
| | | (2) Mendell Benton |
| Carol Annette Joiner | b. 4/28/1963 | |

Lawanda Joiner, born March 5, 1959, is the daughter of Earl (Buddy) Joiner and Winnell (Nell) Soles. Lawanda married William Roger Kitts.

Their child:

Jason Kitts              b. 7/4/1978

Lawanda married the second time to Mendell Benton on April 5, 1982.

Their child:

Mathew Benton          b. 3/12/1988

Shirley Joiner, born September 19, 1941, is the daughter of Arthur Joiner and Alice McNatt. She married Pete Salmon on September 11, 1969. Pete was born June 17, 1946.

Their children:

Steven Salmon           b. 7/27/1970
David Allen Salmon      b. 4/3/1972

Joe Gary Joiner, born July 17, 1943, is the son of Arthur Joiner and Alice McNatt. He married Joyce Powell. Joyce was born in 1946.

Their children:

Joe Gary Joiner, Jr.    b. 6/30/1964
Jimmy Joiner            b. 3/29/1966

Dorothy Sue Joiner, born July 27, 1945, is the daughter of Arthur Joiner and Alice McNatt. She married Lester Bailey on July 4, 1962. Lester was born June 24, 1936.

Their children:

Troy Bailey             b. 12/13/1962     m. Debbie Strickland
Michael Bailey          b. 2/29/1964      m. Barbara Harper
Kenneth Bailey          b. 2/1/1968       m. Georgette Salvo
Joseph Lee Bailey       b. 8/21/1982
Christina Lynn Bailey   b. 5/28/1988

Troy Bailey, born December 13, 1962, is the son of Lester Bailey and Dorothy Sue Joiner. He married Debbie Strickland. Debbie was born April 7, 1963.

Their child:

Anthoney Bailey          b. 6/1986

Michael Bailey, born February 29, 1964, is the son of Lester Bailey and Dorothy Sue Joiner. He married Barbara Harper. Barbara was born November 13, 1967.

Their children:

Justin Bailey            b. 11/21/1986
Jusha Bailey             b. 11/21/1986
Rachelle Bailey          b. 10/1987
Jennifer Bailey          b. 6/15/1988

Kenneth Bailey, born February 1, 1968, is the son of Lester Bailey and Dorothy Sue Joiner. He married Georgette Salvo on August 24, 1988. Georgette was born December 28, 1968.

Their child:

Brittney Bailey          b. 4/12/1989

Arthur Joiner, Jr., born May 7, 1951, is the son of Arthur Joiner and Alice McNatt. He married Carolyn Gibbs in 1971.

Their children:

Tina Joiner              b. 1/23/1972
Elizabeth Jean Joiner    b.                    d. 1987

Arthur Joiner, Jr. has been married several times but is presently married to Roberta Hundley. They were married on November 17, 1989.

# THE OLIF JOINER FAMILY

Olif Joiner, born December 11, 1912, was the daughter of William Joiner and Sabrey Carolina Ryals. She married Plemon Hall, who was the son of Daniel C. Hall and Elizabeth Metts. Olif Joiner died February 13, 1954 of pneumonia. She is buried at the Mt. Union Holiness Baptist (Lax) Church Cemetery.

Their children:

| | | | |
|---|---|---|---|
| Willie Bithie Hall | b. 5/3/1932 | m. | Bernice Rowland |
| Christine Wanda Hall | b. 8/26/1935 | m. | Walter Denzil Gaskins |
| Betty Jean Hall | b. 8/26/1939 | m. | (1) Joe E. Wilson |
| | | | (2) Raymond Pierce Sitton |
| | | | (3) James Dale Cowan |
| Carroll (Carry) Lee Hall | b. 6/24/1941 | m. | (1) Patricia O'Neal |
| | | | (2) Arline Chenault |
| James Lamar Hall | b. 4/22/1948 | m. | (1) Linda Gaskins |
| | | | (2) Barbara June Thompson |
| Baby Hall | b. Died at birth in 1940's | | |

Willie B. Hall, born May 3, 1932, is the son of Plemon Hall and Olif Joiner. He married Bernice Rowland in 1952.

Their children:

| | |
|---|---|
| Doyle Dewayne Hall | b. 3/21/1953 |
| Betty Christine Hall | b. 7/7/1954 |
| Willie B. Hall, Jr. | b. 9/25/1955 |
| Johnnie Carroll Hall | b. 10/15/1956 |
| William Kenneth Hall | b. 11/9/1958 |

Christine Wanda Hall, born August 26, 1935, is the daughter of Plemon Hall and Olif Joiner. She married Walter Denzil Gaskins June 24, 1950.

Their children:

| | | |
|---|---|---|
| Danny Carroll Gaskins | b. 10/7/1951 | m. (1) Sherry Ann Cummings |
| | | (2) Doris Geraldine Walker |
| Alisa Ann Gaskins | b. 6/14/1956 | m. Leonard John Kumpik |

Danny Carroll Gaskins, born October 7, 1951, is the son of Walter Denzil Gaskins and Christine Wanda Hall. He married Sherry Ann Cummings September 23, 1971. They had one child:

Sherry Melissa Gaskins          b. 10/16/1973

Danny married the second time to Doris Geraldine Walker on October 15, 1978. Their children:

Rachel Doris Gaskins          b. 3/31/1980
Danny Carroll Gaskins, Jr.     b. 10/20/1983

Alisa Ann Gaskins, born June 14, 1956, is the daughter of Walter Denzil Gaskins and Christine Wanda Hall. She married Leonard John Kumpik on July 19, 1974.

Their children:

Leonard John Kumpik, Jr.     b. 8/12/1976
Jason Allen Kumpik          b. 7/18/1982

Betty Jean Hall, born August 26, 1939, is the daughter of Plemon Hall and Olif Joiner. She married Joe E. Wilson on July 3, 1954. They have a daughter:

Judy Wilson          b. 7/24/1955          m. Tommy Langston Thompson

Betty Jean Hall married Raymond Pierce Sitton on February 28, 1960.

Their child:

Joyce Sitton       b. 9/9/1958       m. Daniel Levern Johnson

Betty Jean Hall married James Dale Cowan on June 18, 1977. They have no children.

Judy Wilson, born July 23, 1955, is the daughter of Joe E. Wilson and Betty Jean Hall. She married Tommy Langston Thompson on March 17, 1972. Tommy was born January 3, 1953.

Their child:

Shannon Star Thompson       b. 10/2/1972

Joyce Sitton, born September 9, 1958, is the daughter of Raymond Pierce Sitton and Betty Jean Hall. She married Daniel Levern Johnson on October 19, 1975. Daniel was born on November 19, 1952.

Their children:

Paul Daniel Johnson       b. 7/17/1973
(Stepson to Joyce)
Brad Michael Johnson       b. 3/11/1979
Todd Adam Johnson       b. 11/3/1986

Carroll Lee Hall, born June 24, 1941, is the son of Plemon Hall and Olif Joiner. He married Patricia O'Neal on February 5, 1957.

Their children:

Marty Johnathon Hall       b. 9/22/1959       m. (1) Carrie _____
                                              (2) Lisa Roberts
Sandra Kay Hall       b. 10/31/1960
Ramona Gayle Hall       b. 12/1961       m. Robert Brown

Carroll (Carry) Lee Hall married Arline Chenault the second time.

Marty Johnathon Hall, born September 22, 1959, is the son of Carroll Lee Hall and Patricia O'Neal. He married Carrie on June 3, 1977.

The child of Marty Johnathon Hall and his wife, Carrie:

Nancy Kay Hall          b. 8/1/1979

Marty Johnathon Hall married the second time to Lisa Roberts. Lisa was born on August 1, 1955. She had two children:

Machial Arron Ariola       b. 8/25/1976
Brandon Lewis Kelley       b. 9/18/1982

The children of Marty Johnathon Hall and Lisa Roberts:

Marty Johnathon Hall, Jr.   b. 6/14/1986
Dorianne Elise Hall         b. 4/22/1988

Ramona Gayle Hall, born December 1961, is the daughter of Carroll Lee Hall and Patricia O'Neal. She married Robert Brown. Robert was born February 2, 1951.

Their children:

Patricia Brown          b. 11/10/1981
Eric Brown              b. 11/11/1982

James Lamar Hall, born April 22, 1948, is the son of Plemon Hall and Olif Joiner. He married Linda Gaskins on August 3, 1964. Linda was born January 17, 1948 in Berrien County, Ga. Her father was Lawton Gaskins.

Their children:

James Lamar Hall, Jr.    b. 9/7/1965         m. Barbara Jean Lloyd

| | |
|---|---|
| Teresa Malinda Hall | b. 12/19/1966 |
| William David Hall | b. 9/24/1970      m. Misti Collins |
| Judy Lynn Hall | b. 28/1972 |

James Lamar Hall married the second time to Barbara Thompson. Barbara was born June 18, 1957. She had the following children by a previous marriage. They are stepchildren to James Lamar Hall.

| | |
|---|---|
| Christopher Lee Williams | b. 12/26/1976 |
| Dusti Marie Williams | b. 12/2/1979 |

James Lamar Hall, Jr., born September 7, 1965, is the son of James Lamar Hall and Linda Gaskins. James married Barbara Jean Lloyd. She was born August 13, 1966.

Their child:

Brandy Nichole Hall      b. 7/15/1991

Teresa Malinda Hall, born December 19, 1966, is the daughter of James Lamar Hall and Linda Gaskins.

Her child:

Erica Daniell Spivey      b. 5/29/1988

William David Hall, born September 24, 1970, is the son of James Lamar Hall and Linda Gaskins. He married Misti Collins.

Their child:

David James Hall      b. 7/10/1989

## BEN AGIE JOINER FAMILY

Ben Agie Joiner, born December 8, 1908, was the son of William Joiner and Sabrey Carolina Ryals. He was married first to a woman with red hair but her name is not known. There were no children. Ben married Roxie Elizabeth Bell in Berrien County, Ga. on September 28, 1942. Roxie Elizabeth Bell was born June 3, 1912 in Dodge County, Ga. Roxie's parents died when she was very young. She and her sister, Queenie, were raised by their Uncle Norman Bell. Roxie had been married before to a Mr. White. They had no children. He died suddenly.

The children of Ben and Roxie:

| | | |
|---|---|---|
| Randall Joiner | b. 11/3/1943 | |
| Quinnell Joiner | b. 6/7/1948 | m. (1) Lidge Thomas (Melbourne) Mills |
| | | (2) William Terrell Willis |

Roxie Elizabeth Bell White Joiner died August 14, 1969 of a Stroke. She is buried in the Mt. Union Holiness Baptist (Lax) Church Cemetery. Ben Agie Joiner died April 26, 1988 of Cancer of the Kidney. He is also buried in the Mt. Union Holiness Baptist (Lax) Church Cemetery.

Quinnell Joiner, born June 7, 1948, is the daughter of Ben Agie Joiner and Roxie Elizabeth Bell. She married Lidge Thomas (Melbourne) Mills on August 1, 1966. He had 4 children that Quinnell helped to raise.

Their child:

Karron Elizabeth Mills      b. 3/7/1971      m. Denny Lee Varnadoe

Quinnell Joiner married the second time to William Terrell Willis on February 16, 1990.

Karron Elizabeth Mills, born March 7, 1971 is the daughter of Lidge Thomas (Melbourne) Mills and Quinnell Joiner. She married Denny Lee Varnadoe on May of 1989. Denny's parents are Felix and Chung He Varnadoe of Tifton, Ga.

Their child:

DeAnna Leigh Varnadoe      b. 7/31/1990

# THE ELI JOINER FAMILY

Elie Joiner, born May 3, 1910, was the son of William Joiner and Sabrey Carolina Ryals. He married first to Myrtice Smith in Coffee County, Ga. on September 8, 1927. They had one child that was born dead. The child is buried at Mt. Union Holiness Baptist (Lax) Church. Myrtice left Elie and married again. It is not known where she is. He married Doris Jowers on June 15, 1940. Doris was the daughter of Elisha Bijer Jowers and Maudie G. Penn. Doris was born November 8, 1924.

Their children:

| | | |
|---|---|---|
| William Elisha Joiner | b. 9/20/1941 | m. Marie Alice Taylor |
| Raymond Joiner | b. 12/4/1942 | m. Dawn Dixon |
| Sandra Marie Joiner | b. 11/5/1944 | m. Victor Lloyd Slaven |
| Lamar Joiner | b. 8/10/1946  d. 7/18/1988 | m. Daryen Price |
| Johnnie Daryl Joiner | b. 2/13/1950 | m. Patricia Elaine Porter |
| Lucy Dianna Joiner | b. 1/31/1956 | m. Benny Byers |

Elie died in Brandon. Fla. on August 7, 1992. He is buried in Hillsboro Memorial Gardens in Brandon, Fla. He had lived in Brandon, Fla. for several years and worked in the orange groves before retiring. He died of emphysema of the lungs.

William Elisha Joiner, born September 20, 1941, was the son of Elie Joiner and Doris Jowers. He married Marie Alice Taylor on November 17, 1961. Marie was born July 1, 1948.

Their children:

| | |
|---|---|
| Randy William Joiner | b. 3/29/1965 |
| Debira Arline Joiner | b. 1/16/1972 |

Raymond Joiner, born December 4, 1932, is the son of Elie Joiner and Doris Jowers. He married Dawn Dixon on December 29, 1962.

The children of Raymond Joiner and Dawn Dixon:

| | | |
|---|---|---|
| Raymond Joiner, Jr. | b. 7/5/1963 | m. Tami Livezey |
| Donna Jean Joiner | b. 8/26/1964 | m. Randy Michael Tilley |
| April Dawn Joiner | b. 4/11/1971 | |

Raymond Joiner, Jr., born July 5, 1963, was the son of Raymond Joiner and Dawn Dixon. He married Tami Livezey.

Their children:

| | |
|---|---|
| Kayleigh Nicole Joiner | b. 10/18/1987 |
| Jarrett Elie Joiner | b. 5/10/1990 |

Donna Jean Joiner, born August 26, 1964, is the daughter of Raymond Joiner and Dawn Dixon. She married Randy Michael Tilley.

Their child:

Anelia Nerelle Tilley

Sandra Marie Joiner, born November 5, 1944, is the daughter of Elie Joiner and Doris Jowers. She married Victor Lloyd Slaven on February 14, 1964.

Their child:

| | | |
|---|---|---|
| Vickie Dianna Slaven | b. 3/1/1965 | m. (1) Haskell Eugene Chapman |
| | | (2) Steven Ray Connell |
| | | (3) Horst Klaus Bugler |

Vickie Dianna Slaven, born March 1, 1965, is the daughter of Victor Lloyd Slaven and Sandra Marie Joiner. She married Haskell Eugene Chapman on March 1, 1982. Haskell was born April 24, 1964.

Their child:

Deanna Lynn Chapman          b. 8/22/1982

Vickie Dianna Slaven then married Steven Ray Connell on September 29, 1983. Steven was born February 24, 1964. Their child:

Curtis Anthony Connell       b. 8/11/1986

Vickie Dianna Slaven then married Horst Klaus Bugler. He was born August 16, 1958. They have no children.

Lamar Joiner, born August 10, 1946, was the son of Elie Joiner and Doris Jowers. He married Daryen Price. Lamar died July 17, 1988 and is buried in the Hillsboro Memorial Gardens in Brandon, Fla.

Their children:

Regina Michelle Joiner       b. 1/11/1973
Caven Lamar Joiner       b. 5/4/1977

Johnnie Daryl Joiner, born February 13, 1950, is the son of Elie Joiner and Doris Jowers. He married Patricia Elaine Porter. Patricia was born August 23, 1953.

Their children:

Daryl Joiner       b. 9/18/1971
Christy Joiner       b. 12/4/?

Lucy Dianna Joiner, born January 31, 1956, is the daughter of Elie Joiner and Doris Jowers. She married in 1973 to Benny Byers. Benny was born in 1955. Their child:

Treassa Marie Byers       b. 1/20/1975

Lucy married the second time to Randy Sameral Wallace on June 17, 1977. Randy was born June 1, 1957. Their child:

Randell Dewayne Wallace       b. 10/17/1982

Lucy married the third time to Herbert Selye on March 1, 1989. Herbert was born March 30, 1949. They have no children.

# THE BITHIA JOINER FAMILY

Bithia Joiner, born December 1, 1917 in Coffee County, Ga., is the daughter of William Joiner and Sabrey Carolina Ryals. She married George Lemuel Ellis on June 8, 1940 in Berrien County, Ga. George Lemuel Ellis was born April 3, 1920 in Atkinson County, Ga. His parents were Thomas Marion Ellis and Betty Elizabeth Luke.

Their children:

| | | |
|---|---|---|
| Mary Maxine Ellis | b. 10/25/1945 | m. Raymond Gerald Griner |
| George David Ellis | b. 1/20/1949 | m. (1) Connie Lott |
| | | (2) Melvanie Davis |
| | | (3) Mary Kay Herring |
| Charles Wayne Ellis | b. 7/9/1950 | m. Peggy Sumner |
| Pamela Ann Ellis | b. 11/19/1953 | m. (1) Clarence Alton Conger |
| | | (2) Jack Kirkland |
| | | (3) Milledge Wayne Perry |

Bithia continues to live in Willacoochee, Ga. where her brother, Jeff Joiner lives.

George Lemuel Ellis married the second time to Frances Mae Fagon in 1963 in Colorado Springs, Colorado.

Their child:

Donald Regan Ellis        b. 7/29/1962

He was in the Army and stationed in Vietnam when he died of a massive heart attack August 5, 1966. He is buried in the Arlington National Cemetery in Arlington, Va. Frances had two girls at the time she married George. He adopted them but their names are not known to the author.

Mary Maxine Ellis, born October 25, 1945 in Lowndes County, Ga., is the daughter of George Lemuel Ellis and Bithia Joiner. She married Raymond Gerald Griner on November 16, 1962 in Atkinson County, Ga. Raymond Gerald Griner, born November 7, 1944 in Atkinson County, Ga., is the son of Ralph Moye Griner and Louise Spikes.

Their children:

Raymond Gerald Griner, Jr.  b.  10/10/1964        m.  Pamela Harnage (Smith)
Judy Kay Griner              b.  2/7/1966         m.  James Rutherford
Sherry Diane Griner

Raymond Gerald Griner, Jr., was born on October 10, 1964 in Cook County, Ga. He is the son of Raymond Gerald Griner and Mary Maxine Ellis. He married Pamela Harnage on August 11, 1983 in Cook County, Ga. Pamela is the daughter of Howard Harnage and Chaney Fender. She had been married before to E. B. Smith. He had died when she married Raymond Gerald Griner, Jr. She had three daughters by E. B. Smith. One had died at a young age.

Their children:

Penny Smith       b.  12/28/1978
Lorrie Smith      b.  9/29/1981

Judy Kay Griner was born February 7, 1966 in Berrien County, Ga. She is the daughter of Raymond Gerald Griner and Mary Maxine Ellis. She married James Rutherford in Cook County, Ga. on March 15, 1985. James was born March 7, 1961 and is the son of Jack Dewitt Rutherford and Annie Irene Jones.

Their children.

Christopher James Rutherford  b.  4/10/1987
Jonathon Dewitt Rutherford    b.  8/7/1990

George David Ellis was born January 20, 1949 in Witchita Falls, Texas. He is the son of
George Lemuel Ellis and Bithia Joiner. David married first to Connie Lott, who was born
April 26, 1951 in Tift County, Ga., and they had no children. He then married Melvanie
Davis in Willacoochee, Ga. Melvanie was born March 17, 1956 in Coffee County, Ga.
and is the daughter of Melvin Lester Isaac (John) Davis and Alice Poague.

Their children:

| | |
|---|---|
| George David Ellis, Jr. | b. 3/12/1972 |
| John Bradley Ellis | b. 4/4/1974 |
| Mark Anthony Ellis | b. 1/25/1977 |

David then married Mary Kay Herring on March 14, 1987 in Coffee County, Ga. Mary
Kay Herring was born October 21, 1947. Her parents are Donald Lewis Herring and Erby
Mae Hughes. She had four children which David adopted after their marriage.

Their children:

| | | |
|---|---|---|
| Lavada Lynn Ellis | b. 7/7/1973 | m. Shawn Copeland |
| Jeffrey Donald Ellis | b. 11/7/1975 | |
| Johnny Frank Ellis | b. 12/29/1976 | |
| Donald David Ellis | b. 8/9/1984 | |

Lavada Lynn Ellis, born July 7, 1973, is the daughter of George David Ellis and Mary Kay
Herring. She married Shawn Copeland on January 18, 1992 in Coffee County, Ga.

Their child:

Dakota Allen Copeland       b. 5/22/1994

Charles Wayne Ellis was born July 9, 1950 in Witchita Falls, Texas. He is the son of
George Lemuel Ellis and Bithia Joiner. He married Peggy Sumner on December 21, 1969
in Berrien County, Ga. Peggy was born January 30, 1950 in Cook County, Ga., and is the
daughter of Ernest Sumner and Florence Lott.

The children of Charles Wayne Ellis and Peggy Sumner:

Kelly D. Ellis            b. 9/23/1971      m. Doug Faulkner
Michael Ellis         b. 2/5/1975

Kelly D. Ellis, born September 23, 1971 in Berrien County, Ga., is the daughter of Charles Wayne Ellis and Peggy Sumner. She married Douglas A. Faulkner on April 16, 1972 in Berrien County, Ga. Doug was born April 16, 1972 in Berrien County. He is the son of Wayne and Brenda Faulkner. They have no children at this time.

Pamela Ann Ellis, born November 19, 1953 in Lowndes County, Ga., is the daughter of George Lemuel Ellis and Bithia Joiner. Pamela married first to Clarence Alton Conger in Atkinson County, Ga. on July 16, 1971. Clarence was born January 20, 1951. His parents are Clayton and Maedelle Duggan Conger.

The children of Pamela Ann Ellis and Clarence Alton Conger:

Sandy Renee Ellis     b. 9/23/1970    m. Clifford Bradley Lawrence
Tammy Lynn Conger   b. 2/23/1973    m. Mark Anthony Spivey
Gregory Alton Conger  b. 12/18/1977 d. 6/19/1978

Pamela Ann Ellis married the second time to Jack Kirkland on March 14, 1982 in Coffee County, Ga. Jack Kirkland was born October 7, 1942 and died May 22, 1988. They had no children. Pamela then married Milledge Wayne Perry on June 18, 1988 in Coffee County, Ga. Wayne is the son of Milledge Perry and Venice Stone. Wayne was born February 16, 1954.

Their child:

Kayla Marie Perry     b. 10/14/1991

Tammy Lynn Conger was born February 23, 1973 and is the daughter of Clarence Alton Conger and Pamela Ann Ellis. She married Mark Andrew Spivey. Mark was born August 16, 1969. His parents are Jimmy and Jan Spivey.

Their child:

Mark Andrew Spivey    b. 4/30/1992

# THE JEFF JOINER FAMILY

Jeff Joiner, born June 4, 1920, is the son of William Joiner and Sabrey Carolina Ryals. He married Willie Mae McNatt January 21, 1938. Willie Mae is the daughter of Joe Ed McNatt and Mary Emma Luke. She was born October 13, 1920.

Their children:

| | | |
|---|---|---|
| Myrtle Joiner | b. 6/15/1940 | m. James Edgar Rowe |
| Daisy Joiner | b. 12/3/1941 | m. J. T. Chaney |
| Leroy Joiner | b. 2/15/1944 | m. Betty Elizabeth Rowe |
| Bobby Joiner | b. 8/9/1947 | m. Lynda Jean Luke |
| Linda Jane Joiner | b. 5/29/1950 | m. Phillip Wayne Knowles |
| Glenn Joiner | b. 2/21/1956 | m. Pamela Troyneck |
| Katherine Joiner | b. 10/25/1953 | m. James Olin Mizell |

Myrtle Joiner, born June 15, 1940, is the daughter of Jeff Joiner and Willie Mae McNatt. She married James Edgar Rowe on April 3, 1957 in Atkinson County, Ga. James Edgar Rowe is the son of Drew Everette Rowe, Sr.

Their children:

| | | |
|---|---|---|
| Teresa Elaine Rowe | b. 6/10/1960 | m. Huey L. Hancock |
| James (Jimmy)Edgar Rowe, Jr. | b. 2/28/1962 | m. Shirley Diane Douglas |
| Terry Lynn Rowe | b. 1/1/1956 | m. Dan Wade Spell, Jr. |
| Marsha Ann Rowe | b. 3/15/1972 | m. John Robert Clayton |

Teresa Elaine Rowe, born June 10, 1960, is the daughter of James Edgar Rowe and Myrtle Joiner. She married Huey L. Hancock on May 18, 1980. Huey, born August 23, 1960, is the son of Huston Hancock and Grace Soles.

Their children:

| | |
|---|---|
| Traci Nacole Hancock | b. 8/27/1981 |
| Heather Delaine Hancock | b. 8/31/1988 |

James (Jimmy) Edgar Rowe, Jr., born February 28, 1962, is the son of James Edgar Rowe and Myrtle Joiner. He married Shirley Diane Douglas on January 29, 1982. She was born April 14, 1956 in Ben Hill County, Ga.

Their children:

| Jonathan Michael Rowe | b. 11/23/1984 |
| Melaine Diane Rowe | b. 6/18/1986 |

Terry Lynn Rowe, born January 1, 1965, is the daughter of James Edgar Rowe and Myrtle Joiner. She married Dan Wade Spell, Jr. on August 15, 1987 in Cook County, Ga. Dan Wade Spell, Jr. was born September 23, 1964 and is the son of Dan Wade Spell, Sr.

Their child:

| Tara Danielle Spell | b. 7/26/1988 |

Marsha Ann Rowe, born March 15, 1972, is the daughter of James Edgar Rowe and Myrtle Joiner. She married John Robert Clayton on October 21, 1989. John was born December 18, 1966.

Their children:

| Carington Alexis Clayton | b. 5/13/1990 |
| John Zachary Clayton | b. 2/4/1992 |

Daisy Joiner, born December 3, 1941, is the daughter of Jeff Joiner and Willie Mae McNatt. She married J. T. Chaney on October 17, 1958. J. T. Chaney was born December 10, 1937, the son of Ben Chaney and Olive Harper.

Their children:

| John David Chaney | b. 7/31/1959 | m. Sandra Jean Pitts |
| Janice Chaney | b. 11/4/1961 | m. Mark Allen Williams |
| Karen Chaney | b. 2/28/1964 | m. Charles William Paul |
| Timothy Chaney | b. 4/9/1967 | |

John David Chaney, born July 31, 1959, is the son of J. T. Chaney and Daisy Joiner. He married Sandra Jean Pitts on April 26, 1980. Sandra was born June 28, 1962.

Their children:

| | |
|---|---|
| Tiffany Ryan Chaney | b. 5/29/1982 |
| John Mark Chaney | b. 4/20/1985 |

Janice Chaney, born November 4, 1961, is the daughter of J. T. Chaney and Daisy Joiner. She married Mark Allen Williams on March 20, 1988. Mark was born February 3, 1963 and is the son of Charles Williams and Regina Hersey.

Their child:

Samuel Allen Williams             b. 10/12/1991

Leroy Joiner, born February 15, 1944, is the son of Jeff Joiner and Willie Mae McNatt. He married Betty Elizabeth Rowe on October 26, 1963. Betty was born October 26, 1946. She is the daughter of Laster Rowe and Rosie Moore.

Their children:

| | | |
|---|---|---|
| John Russell Joiner | b. 1/14/1967 | m. Angela Renee Mixon |
| Keith Lewis Joiner | b. 5/16/1969 | m. (1) Laura Jo Mancil |
| | | (2) Marcia Lynn Albritton |
| Lee Michelle Joiner | b. 5/26/1971 | m. Ricky McDowell |
| Gina Elizabeth Joiner | b. 3/13/1976 | m. Kevin Vickers |

Keith Lewis Joiner, born May 16, 1969, is the son of Leroy Joiner and Betty Elizabeth Rowe. He married Laura Jo Mancil on June 11, 1988.

Their child:

Chadwick Hiram Joiner          b. 5/6/1989

Keith Lewis Joiner, born May 16, 1969, married the second time to Marcia Lynn Albritton on May 12, 1990.

Their child:

Tyler William Joiner        b. 10/27/1990

Lee Michelle Joiner, born May 26, 1971, is the daughter of Leroy Joiner and Betty Elizabeth Rowe. She married Ricky McDowell on February 24, 1990. Ricky was born August 1, 1971.

Their child:

Jonathon Grandville McDowell    b. 9/19/1993

Gina Elizabeth Joiner, born March 13, 1976, is the daughter of Leroy Joiner and Betty Elizabeth Rowe. She married Kevin Vickers on March 18, 1994.

Bobby Joiner, born August 9, 1946, is the son of Jeff Joiner and Willie Mae McNatt. He married Lynda Jean Luke on March 17, 1964. Jean is the daughter of John Luke and was born May 9, 1948.

Their children:

| | | |
|---|---|---|
| Janet Joiner | b. 11/13/1965 | m. (1) John Gile Mizell |
| | | (2) Terry Crews |
| Connie Joiner | b. 10/9/1966 | m. Rodney Bryan |
| Michael Joiner | b. 6/9/1967 | m. Patricia Ann Dees |
| Amy Joiner | b. 3/3/1978 | |

Janet Joiner, born November 13, 1965, is the daughter of Bobby Joiner and Lynda Jean Luke. She married the first time to John Gile Mizell.

Their children:

| | |
|---|---|
| Jessica Renee Mizell | b. 4/7/1982 |
| Sara Nicole Mizell | b. 5/1/1983 |

Janet Joiner, born November 13, 1965, married the second time to Terry Crews.

Their child:

Matthew Aaron Crews        b. 10/26 /1988

Connie Joiner, born October 9, 1966, is the daughter of Bobby Joiner and Lynda Jean Luke. She married Rodney Bryan.

Their child:

Joshua Nathaniel Bryan        b. 8/2/1985

Michael Joiner, born June 9, 1967, is the son of Bobby Joiner and Lynda Jean Luke. He married Patricia Ann Dees on June 18, 1988.

Their child:

Carrie Lynn Joiner        b. 8/4/1989

Michael Joiner, born June 9, 1967, also had a twin daughter and son by his cousin, Rachel L. Joiner, who is the daughter of Leon and Kathy Joiner. They never married.

Their children:

Taylor L. Joiner        b. 11/17/1993
Tylor L. Joiner        b. 11/17/1993

Glynn Joiner, born February 22, 1952, is the son of Jeff Joiner and Willie Mae McNatt. He married Pamela Troyneck. on May 22, 1970. Pam was born February 29, 1952.

Their child:

Angela Gwyn Joiner        b. 5/24/1972        m. Travis Tate Griffin

Angela Gwyn Joiner, born May 24, 1972, is the daughter of Glynn Joiner and Pamela Troyneck. She married Travis Tate Griffin on September 18, 1993. Tate was born on December 22, 1969.

Linda Jane Joiner, born May 29, 1950, is the daughter of Jeff Joiner and Willie Mae McNatt. Linda married Phillip Wayne Knowles on August 2, 1968. Phillip was born April 21, 1947.

Their children:

| | |
|---|---|
| Cynthia Lynn Knowles | b. 10/19/1971 |
| Selena Denise Knowles | b. 10/14/1975 |

Katherine Joiner, born October 25, 1953, is the daughter of Jeff Joiner and Willie Mae McNatt. She married James Olin Mizell on December 10, 1970. James was born March 15, 1950.

Their children:

| | |
|---|---|
| James Bradley Mizell | b. 5/10/1971 |
| John Damon Mizell | b. 5/10/1972 |
| Roy Jeffery Mizell | b. 6/8/1977 |
| Vickie Lynn Mizell | b. 8/25/1981 |

James Bradley Mizell, born May 10, 1971, is the son of James Olin Mizell and Katherine Joiner. He has one child. He is not married to the mother.

His child:

| | |
|---|---|
| Haley Marie Zimmerman | b. 7/28/1990 |

# THE ROSCOE JOINER FAMILY

Roscoe Joiner, born January 2, 1923 in Coffee County, Ga., was the son of William Joiner and Sabrey Carolina Ryals. He married Rita Chaput. Rita was the daughter of Joseph Chaput and Malvina Demaris. She was born 1927 in PLainfield Co., Conn.

Their children:

| Richard Joiner | b. 3/26/1946 | m. Carol Ann Partridge |
| Marjorie Joiner | b. 6/10/1947 | m. (1) Joseph George W. Dube, Sr. |
| | | (2) Marshall Black |
| Glenda Sue Joiner | b. 10/27/1950 | m. Roger Nelson Partridge, Sr. |
| Leon Joiner | b. 9/1/1949 | m. (1) Kathy |
| | | (2) Sherry |
| Larry Joiner | b. 10/29/1952 | |
| Charles Edward Joiner | b. 1/7/1955 | m. Joyce Mary Angell |
| Ronald Joiner | b. 8/3/1956 | m. Debbie |
| Rebecca A. Joiner | b. 2/22/1960 | m. Charles Raymond Yawn |
| Lisa Denise Joiner | b. 2/22/1964 | m. Jessie Charles Yawn |

Rita Chaput Joiner died at Tift General Hospital in Tifton, Ga. on April 21, 1991. She is buried at Mt. Union (Lax) Holiness Baptist Church Cemetery. Roscoe Joiner died November 15, 1992. He is also buried at Mt. Union (Lax) Holiness Baptist Church Cemetery.

Richard Joiner, born March 26, 1946 in Alapaha, Ga., is the son of Roscoe Joiner and Rita Chaput. He married Carol Ann Partridge on May 29, 1965. Carol was born January 30, 1947.

Their children:

| Richard Joiner, Jr. | b. 3/18/1966 | |
| Laurie Ann Joiner | b. 8/24/1967 | m. Daniel Wyman Converse |
| Nancy Joiner | b. 1/30/1971 | |
| Randall Scott Joiner | b. 9/27/1972 | |

Marjorie Joiner, born June 10, 1947, is the daughter of Roscoe Joiner and Rita Chaput. She married Joseph George W. Dube, Sr. the first time.

Their children:

| | | |
|---|---|---|
| Rita Marie Dube | b. 6/18/1968 | m. Steve Rudolph |
| Joseph George W. Dube, Jr. | b. 7/4/1969 | m. Monica Vickers |
| Marci Elizabeth Dube | b. 9/19/1975 | |

Marjorie Joiner married the second time to Marshall Black. They had no children.

Rita Marie Dube, born June 18, 1968, is the daughter of Marjorie Joiner and Joseph George W. Dube, Sr. She married Steve Rudolph.

Their child:

Katherine Rudolph          b. 01/1991

Marci Elizabeth Dube, born September 19, 1975, is the daughter of Marjorie Joiner and Joseph George W. Dube, Sr. She was married but her husband's name is unknown.

Her child:

Kara M. Dube          b. 8/2/1992

Glenda Sue Joiner, born October 27, 1950 in Willacoochee, Ga., is the daughter of Roscoe Joiner and Rita Chaput. She married Roger Nelson Partridge on May 17, 1968.

Their children:

| | |
|---|---|
| Roger Nelson Partridge, Jr. | b. 5/16/1969 |
| Melissa Lee Partridge | b. 11/18/1970 |
| Candy Ann Partridge | b. 9/8/1973 |
| Kerry Lyn Partridge | b. 3/11/1976 |
| Amanda Jean Partridge | b. 6/20/1983 |

Lisa Denise Joiner, born March 27, 1964, is the daughter of Roscoe Joiner and Rita Chaput. She married Jessie Charles Yawn August 5, 1983.

Their children:

| | |
|---|---|
| Jessie Brian Yawn | b. 6/13/1984 |
| Ashley Marie Yawn | b. 2/12/1988 |

Charles Edward Joiner, born January 7, 1955, is the son of Roscoe Joiner and Rita Chaput. He married Joyce Mary Angell. Joyce was born September 12, 1956.

Their children:

| | |
|---|---|
| Gary Micheal Joiner | b. 7/9/1976 |
| Robert Lee Joiner | b. 4/21/1978 |

Rebecca A. Joiner, born February 22, 1960, is the daughter of Roscoe Joiner and Rita Chaput. She married Charles Raymond Yawn. Raymond was born February 1, 1956.

Their child:

| | |
|---|---|
| Sue A. Yawn | b. 11/16/1981 |
| Charles Roscoe Yawn | b. 4/29/1994 |

Leon Joiner, born September 1, 1949, is the son Roscoe Joiner and Rita Chaput. He married Kathy. Her last name is unknown.

Their children:

| | |
|---|---|
| Pauline Joiner | b. about 1969 |
| Christine Joiner | b. about 1971 |
| Rachel L. Joiner | b. 5/24/1973 |
| Barbara Jean Joiner | b. 8/20/1974 |

Leon Joiner married the second time to Sherry. Her last name is unknown. They have no children.

Rachel L. Joiner, born May 24, 1973, is the daughter of Leon Joiner and first wife, Kathy. She had twins by her cousin, Michael Joiner, son of Bobby Joiner and Lynda Jean Luke.

Their children:

Taylor L. Joiner      b. 11/17/1993
Tylor L. Joiner       b. 11/17/1993

Ronald Joiner, born August 3, 1956 in Atkinson County, Ga., is the son of Roscoe Joiner and Rita Chaput. He married Debbie. Her birthdate and maiden name are unknown.

Their child:

Katie Joiner

# INDEX

BRIGMON, Lindsey 27.

BROOKS, Virginia Lee 69,70.

BROWN, Cranston 69,70, Eric 80, Fred J. 26, H. I. 26, Patricia 80, Robert 79, 80, Sarah 60, Vienna Jane 65.

BROWNING, Emeline M. 52, Green H. 52, Missouri F. 52.

BRYAN, Joshua Nathaniel 94, Rodney 93, 94.

BUGLER, Horst Klaus 84, 85.

BURCH, Ann Jane 23, Charles 54, Christian 53, 54, Reuben Flournoy 49.

BURNETT, Diane 29, 30.

BURT, William 59.

BUTLER, Hannah 47, 48.

BYERS, Benny 83, 85, Treassa Marie 85.

CADWELL, Aaron 47, 48, Abigail 47, Allen 48, 49, Charlotte 49, Christian 48, Edward 47, Elizabeth 47, Hannah 47, Hanna 47, James 47, 48, Jonathan 48, Jonath 47, Lois Penelope 48, Lois 48, Louis 48, Margaret 49, Martin 48, Mary 47, 48, Matthew 47, Melhit-a'bell 47, Moses 47, 48, Olie 48, Peletiah 48, Rebecca 49, 53, 63, 64, Rhoda 48, Samuel 47, Sarah 48, Thomas 47, 48, Timothy 48.

CALHOUN, Angres 22.

CARR, Lige 56.

CARTER, Christy Elaine 30, David 26, 27, Dustin Grant 19, Earl S. 29, 30, Early Johnson 34, Floye 27, Hubert 27, Joshua Todd 19, Lizzie 27, Lois 27, Lula 27, Maggie 27, Marci Denise 30, Michael Earl 30, Ocie C. 34, Opal 27, Paul E. 27, Ruth 27, Sol 27, Troy David, Jr. 19, Troy David 18, 19, William 27.

CARVER, Allen 39, Alvin 50, Anna Belle 34, Brazien (Brazie) 34, 35, Dennis Wesley 34, Estelle 34, Fannie 10, 50, James D. 38, 39, James L. 50, Jimmie Sue 39, John R. 10, Johnnie Brazie 34, Joseph 34, 50, Lawton 50, Lenny 74, Leroy 34, Lithie 50, Mahala 50, Mary Jane (Mollie) 34, Melvin Ryals 34, Minnie 10, Needham 17, 50, Olif Mabel 34, 35, Polly 11, 17, 50, Rachel 39, 40, Raymond, Jr. 34, Raymond 33, 34, 35, Sampson Brazwell 34, Samuel 10, Silas 4, 10, Thomas 10, Tom 50, Walter 50, Winnie Grace 34.

CHAIRES, Ashley Adelle 31, Carl David 30, 31, Carl Hendrick 29, 30, 31, Justin Carl 31, Kenneth Wayne 30, Margaret Ann 30, 31.

CHAMPION, James 46, John 65.

CHANEY, Ben 91, Billy, 43, Bob 43, Dixie 43, Duanne 70, J. T. 90, 91, 92, Janice 91, 92, John David 91, 92, John Mark 92, Karen 91, Landon Trent 69, Larry 69, 70, M. L. 42, 43, Marci 70, Nell 43, Ronnie Keith, Jr. 69, Ronnie Keith 68, 69, Tiffany Ryan 92, Timothy 91.

CHAPMAN, Deanna Lynn 84, Haskell Eugene 84.

CHAPPELL, Elma R. 33.

CHAPUT, Joseph 96, Rita 11, 96, 97, 98, 99.

CHENAULT, Arline 77, 80.

CHILDS, Edith 22, 23.

CLARK, Charlotte 22, 23, 24, 26, 32, 52, Elijah, Jr. 23, 51, 52, 62, Elijah 51, 52, Gibson 51, John P. 52, John 51, Joseph 52, Michael 51, Mollie 54, Nimrod 52, Oran 52, Patrick 52, Sarah 51, Sharlotte 52, Susanna 51, William 51, 52.

CLARKE, Elizabeth 51, Frances 51, Nancy 51, Polly 51, Susan 51.

CLAYTON, Carington Alexis 91, John Robert 90, 91, John Zachary 91.

CLIETT, Amanda Lee 30, Angela 29, 30, Bradley Felton III 29, 30, Bradley Felton IV 30, Bradley Felton Jr. 28, 29, 30, Deborah 29, Donald 29, Julie Marie 30, Marcus Stanford 29, 30.

COLEMAN, Agnes 54, Alfred T. 53, Anna 54, Arthur 55, Bartemus T. 53, 55, Charles Andrew 54, Clara 55, Docia 54, Dr. Warren Ashley 55, Elisha 55, Elvenia 56, General Lee 54, 55, General Robert Lee 53, Georgia Belle 54, Hattie 54, Henry Clay 55, Isaac 56, James Andrew 53, 54, Joel Franklin 53, 55, Joel Vernon 55, John Andrew 54, Kenneth 55, Levi Samuel 54, Lucinda 63, 64, Lugenia 56, Mamie Ethel 56, Martha Caroline 56, Martha J. 53, Mary Eliza 53, Mary Louisa 55, Mary 53, 55, Nancy Ann 64, Nancy Jane 53, Nancy Rosella 56, Nannie 55, Oeida 55, Priscilla 55, Roxie Rebecca 23, 32, 33, 34, 35, 38, 42, 53, 66, Sabra Caroline 53, Sadie 54, Samantha Priscilla 55, Sarah Lucretia 56, Thomas Andrew 55, Wade Andy 56, Wade Hampton, Jr. 55, Wade Hampton 53, 54, Walter Jackson 55, William Andrew 32, 53, 54, 55, 63, 64, William C. 53, William J. 63, William Levi 56, William Thomas 54, Zuma 56, Zuna 56.

COLLINS, Misti 81.

CONGER, Clarence Alton 86, 89, Gregory Alton 89, Tammy Lynn 89.

CONNELL, Curtis Anthony 85, Steven Ray 84, 85.

CONNER, Eliza 22, 24, James Gassaway 22, Lucy Ann 22, Marie McDonald 23, Rev. Wilson 23.

CONVERSE, Daniel Wyman 96.

COOK, Mary 23.

COPELAND, Dakota Allen 88, Shawn 88.

CORBITT, Janie Avanell 36.

COUEY, Sybyle 55.

COWAN, James Dale 77.

COX, Amanda Marie 68.

CREWS, Matthew Aaron 94, Terry 93, 94.

CROCKER, William 62.

CROWELL, John 65.

CRUMPTON, Nora 64.

CUMMINGS, Sherry Ann 78.

DARSEY, Dora 56.

DAVIS, Amanda 45, Annie 45, Catherine 62, Dale 28, Dean 28, Ethel 35, 36, Henry 35, Hiram (Buster), Jr. 27, 28, Melvanie 86, 88, Melvin Lester Isaac (John) 88, Sallie 34.

DAY, Jerry 39.

DEES, Patricia Ann 93, 94.

DEMARIS, Melvina 96.

DIETZEL, Johanna Hildegarde 42, 44.

DIXON, Dawn 83, 84.

DOUGLAS, Shirley Diane 90, 91.

DUBE, Joseph George W., Jr. 97, Joseph George W., Sr. 96, 97, Kara M. Dube, 97, Marci Elizabeth 97, Rita Marie 97.

DUGGAN, Jennifer 16, Maedelle 89.

DUKES, Christine 40.

EASON, Dempsey 57, Edith 3, 57, Elizabeth 57, Eunice 57, Isaias 57, John 57, Mary 57, Milley 3, 57, Ruth 57, Samuel 3, 57, William 57.

EDWARDS, Christine 55.

ELEY, Eley 2.

ELLIS, Charles Wayne 86, 88, 89, Clarence 42, Donald David 88, Donald Regan 86, George David, Jr. 88, George David 86, 88, George Lemuel 11, 86, 87, 88, 89, Jeffrey Donald 88, John Bradley 88, Johnny Frank 88, Kelley D. 89, Lavada Lynn 88, Mark Anthony 88, Mary Maxine 86, 87, Michael 89, Pamela Ann 86, 89, Sandy Renee 89, Temperance 46, Thomas Marion 86, Wiley 33, 42.

EPPS, Francis 21, Mary 20, 21.

EVANS, Joseph H. 53.

FAGON, Frances Mae 86.

FALES, Seaborn 45.

FAULKNER, Brenda 89, Douglas A. 89, Wayne 89.

FENDER, Carl 6, Chaney 87.

FLETCHER, Joseph, Sr. 45, Sarah 45, 46.

FLOYD, Willie 56.
FOOT, Mary 48.
FORDHAM, Iverson Conner 56.
FOWLER, Fred 10.
FRANCES, Mary 10.
FUSSELL, Bernie 18, Lamar 18, Twyla Elaine 18, 19.
FUTCH, Dobbin 26, Governor 26, Otis 26, Pearl 26, W. R. 25, 26.
GARRETT, Morris 34.
GASKINS, Alisa Ann 78, Danny Carroll, Jr. 78, Danny Carroll 78, Lawton 7, 80, Linda
77, 80, 81, Patricia 6, 7, Rachel Doris 78, Sherry Melissa 78, Walter Denzil 77, 78.
GAY, Theo 55.
GEIGER, Rilda 41.
GILLESPIE, Myrtle 12, 16.
GORDON, Betty 55.
GRAHAM, Pauline 55, Pearl 54, Thomas 65.
GRANTHAM, Dawn 15, Robbie 14, 15.
GRAY, Amanda L. 9, Lewis, Jr. 8, 9, Odessa V. 9.
GRIFFIN, Ann 3, Henrietta 1, James 24, Mary 24, Travis Tate 94, 95, Terri Lee 29.
GRINER, Adlai B. 25, Agnes Virginia 25, 26, Annie Laura 25, Carmen 25, Daniel Newton
24, 25, Daniel 24, Dorothy 25, Edna Eleanor 24, Ernest C. 25, F. P. 25, Fairy 25, Frances
25, Ida C. 24, James Hasty 25, Jasper Martin 24, Judy Kay 87, Mamie 25, Martin Jasper
24, Oliver C. 24, Ralph Moye 87, Raymond Gerald, Jr. 87, Raymond Gerald 86, 87,
Robert Bruce 24, 25, Robert W. 25, Sarah 25, Sherry Diane 87, Vera 25.
GUERSEY, Charles 18.
GUESS, Ollie Mae 38, 40.
GUEST, Jack 33, 34, Maude Estelle 34, Nancy 34, Polly Ann 33.
HAISLIP, Tom 55.
HALL, Betty Christine 77, Betty Jean 78, 78, 79, Bobby 12, 14, Brandi Nichole 81,
Carroll Lee 77, 79, 80, Chester 12, 16, Christine Wanda 77, 78, Daniel C. 77, David
James 81, Delphia 60, Dorianne Elise 80, Doyle Dewayne 77, Glenn 13, James Lamar, Jr.
80, 81, James Lamar 77, 80, 81, Johnnie Carroll 77, Judy Lynn 81, Marty Johnathon, Jr.
80, Marty Johnathon 79, 80, Nancy Kay 80, Plemon 11, 77, 78, 79, 80, Ramona Gayle 79,
80, Ruby 12, 13, Sandra Kay 79, Teresa Malinda 81, Thomas 22, Willaim David 81,
William Kenneth 77, Willie B., Jr. 77, Willie Bithie 77.
HAMILTON, Benjamin 49, Donald 39, Phoebe 59, Ronald 39.
HANCOCK, Heather Delaine 90, Huey L. 90, Huston 90, Traci Nacole 90.

HARNAGE, Howard, 87, Pamela 87.

HARPER, Barbara 75, 76, Edsel 12, 13, 14, 15, James E. 15, James Horace 14, 15, Jean 14, Jessica R. 15, Louise 6, 7, 8, Mathias 9, Maudine 6, 9, 10, Olive 91, Perry 6. Retha Dean 14, 15.

HARRELL, Ann 10, 45, 46, 60, Asa 58, 59, Della 45, Elizabeth 60, Esther 59, Ethelred 59, Frances 58, Francis 4, 58, Jacob 58, 59, Jane 4, 58, 60, Jasper 58, John James 59, Levi 58, 59, Lewis 58, Lovett 5, 45, 59, 60, Mary Jane 59, Mary 60, Maude 39, Millie Ann 59, Pinkie 46, Priscilla 60, Samuel 59, Sarah 60, Susan 60, William I. 58, William 60, Willis P. 59.

HARRISON, Mary 60.

HATTAWAY, Eleanor D. 67, 68, 69.

HENDERSON, Deborah Elaine 31, Herman Sheldon 29, 31, 32, Mary 23, Pamela Margarette 31, 32.

HENDLEY, Sophia 59.

HERRING, Donald Lewis 88, Mary Kay 86, 88.

HERSEY, Regina 92.

HIGHSMITH, Ronald Troy 68, 69.

HIGHTOWER, Cecil 54, Josh 46, Lizzie 6.

HILL, Gregory Webster 70, Gregory 69, 70.

HOLT, Elizabeth 58.

HOLTON, Estelle 34.

HONORS, Kim 73, 74.

HOOKER, Elizabeth 21.

HOPE, Angela 18.

HORNER, James 6.

HORTON, Amanda L. 15, Danny T. 15, Darrell A. 15, Darrell 14, 15, Kelly M. 15, Laura M. 15, Mathew D. 15.

HOWARD, Carline 6, 8.

HUDSON, William 62.

HUGHES, Erby 88.

HULSEY, Alvin 42.

HUNDLEY, Roberta 73, 76.

HURSEY, Sellers 5.

HURST, Aaron 46, Jane 46, Lawrence 46, Mary Ann 46, William R. 46, William 45, 46.

HUTCHESON, Amy 42, 43, Arlie Helen 42, 43, Culas W., Jr. 44, Culas W. 42, 44, Effie 42, 43, Heidi 44, Lynn 44, Mark 44, Valeree 42, William Bryant 42, Wiley 33, 42, 43, 44.

HUTTO, Henry 4, Nancy 4, 5, 10, Polly 4.

ISHAM, Ann 21, Henry, Jr. 21, Henry 21, Mary 21.

IVENS, Richard Warren 70, Richard 69, 70.

JACKSON, Nancy 62.

JOHNSON, Brad Michael 79, Carly Jeanette 31, Cody Lee 69, Daniel Levern 79, Don 30, 31, Gary Lee 68, 69, James Howard, Jr. 29, 32, Lauren Michelle 31, Marcia Lynn 32, Paul Daniel 79, Todd Adam 79.

JOINER, Albert 9, Alene 6, Allen 4, 10, 11, 12, 17, 45, 66, Amy 93, Angela Gwyn 94, 95, Angela 7, Annie Belle 11, April Dawn 84, April 71, Arlene 6, 8, Arthur, Jr. 73, 76, Arthur 11, 66, 73, 74, 75, 76, Aubrey 17, 18, Barbara Ann 69, 70, Ben Agie 11, 66, 82, Benjamin 4, Bennie David 73, Bithia 11, 66, 86, 87, 88, 89, Blair Howell 8, Barbara Jean 98, Bobby 90, 93, 94, 99, Brad 70, Brandie 8, Brenda 7, Carol Annette 74, Carrie Lynn 94, Cathy Jo 68, Caven Lamar 85, Chadwick Hiram 92, Charles Edward 96, 98, Charley 5, 10, Charlie 69, 70, Ronnie Chase 8, Cheryl 18, Christie Kay 71, Christine 98, Christy 85, Chrystal 8, Connie 93, 94, Cornelius 3, Daisy 90, 91, 92, Daniel 4, Darrell 69, 71, Daryl 85, David William 68, David 9, Debira Arline 83, Debra Jean 68, 69, Derrick William 8, Donna Jean 84, Dorothy Sue 73, 75, 76, Dorothy 10, E. L. 9, Earl 73, 74, 75, Elie 11, 66, 83, 84, 85, Elizabeth Jean 76, Elizabeth 5, Ellen Rebecca 68, 69, Gaines 5, 6, 8, 10, Gary Michael 98, Gellet 10, Gene Evelyn 7, George Samuel 73, Gerald 6, Gina Elizabeth 92, 93, Glenda Sue 96, 97, Glenn, Jr. 71, Glenn 69, 71, Glynn 90, 94, 95, Harden 4, 5, 60, Hardy, Jr. 5, Harold William 6, 8, Harvey 5, Harvie 6, 7, 8, Herbert 9, Hiram, 9, Ivey Larry 69, 70, Ivey Warren 67, 69, 70, 71, Ivey 5, Jacob 4, 57, James Lamar 6, 8, James 73, Janet Marie 67, 68, Janet 93, 94, Janice Jessica 18, Jarrett Elie 84, Jason Todd 70, Jeff 11, 66, 86, 91, 92, 93, 94, 95, Jennifer Michelle 70, Jennifer 8, Jimmy 75, Joe Gar, Jr. 75, Joe Gary 73, 75, John Russell 92, John William 67, 68, Johnnie Daryl 83, 85, Joyce 6, 8, Judy Delois 68, Julie Michele 68, Katherine 90, 95, Katie 99, Kayleigh Nicole 84, Keith Lewis 92, 93, Kimberly Elaine 8, Lamar 70, 83, 85, Larry Joshua 70, Larry 96, Laura Elizabeth 11, 12, 16, 17, Laurie Ann 96, Lawanda 74, 75, Lee Michelle 92, 93, Leon 94, 96, 98, 99, Leroy 90, 92, 93, Lester 6, Linda Jane 90, 95, Lisa Ann 70, Lisa Denise 96, 98, Lorene 18, Lounita Ann 7, Lowe 5, 9, Lucy Dianna 83, 85, Lucy 5, Marjorie 96, 97, Mary Alice 73, 74, Mary Allison 70, Mary J. 5, Mary Nell 69, 70, Melissa (Wright) 8, 9, Melissa 6, Michael 93, 94, 99, Michael Joseph 67, 68, Minnie Dell 5, Mose 11, 66, 67, 68, 69, Myrtle 90, 91, Nancy Jane 4, 10, Nancy 96, Olif 11, 66, 77, 78, 79, 80, Opal 10, Orvel 18, Pauline 98, Peggy Lynn 68, 69, Preston 10, Quinnell 82, Rachel L. 94, 99, Randall Scott 96, Randall 82, Randy William 83, Randy 71, Raymond, Jr. 84, Raymond 83, 84, Rebecca A. 96, 98,

Regina Michelle 85, Richard, Jr. 96, Richard 96, Richmond 5, Robert Lee 98, Robert 4, 5, 67, Ronald 96, 99, Ronnie Chase 8, Roscoe 11, 66, 96, 97, 98, 99, Roy Dale 18, Roy 9, Ruby 9, Sandra Kay 68, Sandra Marie 83, 84, Sarah 4, Shilo 8, Shirley 73, 75, Sophia 4, Spencer Lee 67, 68, 69, Stephen 7, Stevie 7, T. J. 11, 12, 33, Taylor L. 94, 99, Teresa Ann 18, Thomas J. J. 4, 5, 10, Thomas 4, 11, 17, 50, Tina 76, Tommy 69, 70, Tyler William 93, Tylor L. 94, 99, Vivian 17, 19, Walter Lee 18, Walter 17, 18, 19, Warren 5, 10, Wilbert 17, 18, William Elisha 83, William 4, 5, 6, 11, 33, 66, 67, 72, 73, 77, 82, 83, 86, 90, 96, Willie Lee 11, 66, 72.

JONES, Annie Irene 87, Elizabeth 59, James 54.

JOWERS, Doris 11, 83, 84, 85, Elisha Bijer 83.

JOYNER, Abraham 1, Ann 2, Bridgeman 1, Burrell 3, Cornelius 3, Drewry 3, Elizabeth 2, 3, Giles 2, Hardy 3, Israel 1, 2, Jacob 3, 4, Jethro 2, John 1, 3, Jordan 3, Joseph 1, Lawrence 2, Lewis 2, 3, Mary 3, Moses 2, Nancy Ann 3, Nathan 3, Theophilus 1, Thomas, Jr. 1, Thomas 1, 3, William A. 3, William W. 2, 3, William Jr. 1, 2, William 1, 2, 3.

KEEN, Elizabeth 58, 59, John 59.

KELLEY, Brandon Lewis 80.

KENNON, Elizabeth 21.

KIRKLAND, Benajah 45, Jack 86, 89, Manassa 27, Mollie 54, Nannie Elizabeth 54.

KITCHENS, Richard 73, 74.

KITE, Carolene 40.

KITTS, Jason 75, William Roger 74, 75.

KNOWLES, Cynthia Lynn 95, Phillip Wayne 90, 95, Selena Denise 95.

KUMPIK, Jason Allen 78, Leonard John, Jr. 78, Leonard John 78.

LANIER, Elizabeth 45.

LANKFORD, Chester, 17, 19, James 60.

LAWRENCE, Ann 2, 3, Clifford Bradley 89, Sally 42.

LEDON, Hazel Mae 12.

LEE, Amy Ann 43, Ann 55, Brenda Joy 43, Polly 6, Susanna L. 63, 64, W. Ottis 42, 43, Wayne 43, William 64.

LEIGH, Emily 3.

LESLIE, Mae 17, 18.

LITTLEBERRY, Elizabeth 21.

LIVEZEY, Tami 84.

LIVINGSTON, Drucilla 65, Henry 65, Laura 55, Love 55, Martin 64, Sybil Ann 64.

LLOYD, Barbara Jean 80, 81.

LONG, Anderson 61, Benjamin 61, Betty 61, Bromfield 61, Elizabeth 61, Evans 61, 62, Frances 62, Gabriel 60, John 60, Lucinda 62, Lunceford 62, Margaret 51, 52, 62, Mary 60, 62, Milly 60, Nancy 60, Nicholas 60, Nimrod Washington 62, Nimrod 60, Peggy 62, Polly 62, Reuben 60, Samuel 60, Sarah Ann 62, Thomas 60.
LOTT, Annie 45, 46, Beulah 11, 72, Connie 86, 88, Florence 88.
LOVELESS, Sallie 54.
LUKE, Betty Elizabeth 86, John 93, Lynda Jean 90, 93, 94, 99, Mary Emma 73, 90.
MANCIL, Breana 39, Jeana 14, 15, Laura Jo 16, 92, Mark 39, Noah, Jr. 39, Noah 39, Shannon 39.
MANN, Elinor 1.
MATHIS, Barbara 6, 8.
MAYO, Ann 1.
McDonald, Auston 41, Willie Mae Carver McDonald 28, 29.
MCDOWELL, Jonathon Grandville 93, Ricky 92, 93.
MCGEE, David 36, Donald 36, W. D. 36.
MCKINNON, Hubert 27, 28, Jessie 28, Patsy 28.
MCLARTY, Alan Dougald 31, Allison Jeanette 31, Stephanie Elaine 31.
MCLEAN, Linda 69, 70.
MCLEOD, Clarence 55, Linnie 46.
MCMILLAN, Daniel "Babe" 28, Margaret 26, 28, 29, 30, 31, 32.
MCNATT, Alice 11, 73, 74, 75, 76, Joe Ed 73, 90, Willie Mae 11, 90, 91, 92, 93, 94, 95.
MERRITT, Kathy A. 14, 15, Lucy 17, 18, 19, Rebecca 38.
MERRY, Sarah 47, 48.
METTS, Amanda 40, Beulah 38, 39, Blannie 38, 41, Bobby 9, Carswell 40, 41, Dan 38, 40, Donnie 41, Dot 17, Earnest 9, Elias 32, 38, 39, 40, 41, Elizabeth 77, Elton 38, 40, 41, Geneva 41, Henry 38, Johnny 40, Lonnie 6, 9, Lucy 41, Macajah 38, Margie 41, Myrtle 41, Pat 17, Richard 12, 17, Robert 41, Roger Wayne, Jr. 40, Roger Wayne 40, Roy Earl 40, William 38, 41.
MILLS, Karron Elizabeth 82, Lidge Thomas 82, Osbon J. 26, Rebecca Ann 23, 26, Roger 12, 14.
MIXON, Angela Renee 92.
MIZELL, James Bradley 95, James Olin 90, 95, Jessica Renee 93, John Damon 95, John Gile 93, Roy Jeffery 95, Sara Nicole 93, Vickie Lynn 95.
MOORE, Cecil 56, Emma 65, Mitchell 32, Rosie 92, Sherrie 32.
MORELAND, Tuttle 62.

MORGAN, Alma 36, Marvin 36.
MORRIS, Vera 38, 40, 41.
MORRISON, Marie 54.
MOUNGER, Edward 51.
MOZO, A. Leon 55.
MULLIS, Etta 65, Wesley 55.
MURPHY, Carolyn 36.
NASH, Alif L. 24, Ann Eliza 24, James 24, John W. 24, Mariah L. 24, Mary Jane 24, Newton 23, 24, Olive 24, 25.
NICHOLSON, Samantha Ann Francis 63, 64, 65.
NIPPER, Georgiann 5, 6, 9, 10, Mary Ellen 5, 10, Susan 5, 45, 59, 60.
O'NEAL, Annie 12, 13, 14, 16, Patricia 77, 79, 80, Willis 12.
O'STEEN, Kacie Amanda 13, Kendra Leigh 13, Kenneth 13.
OWENS, Elizabeth 58, John 62.
PARTRIDGE, Amanda Jean 97, Candy Ann 97, Carol Ann 96, Kerry Lyn 97, Melissa Lee 97, Roger Nelson, Jr. 97, Roger Nelson, Sr. 96, 97.
PAUL, Charles William 91.
PEACOCK, Oppie Lee 55.
PENNY, Sarah 10.
PERRIN, Richard 20.
PERRY, Emma Eunice 54, Kayla Marie 89, Milledge Wayne 86, 89, Milledge 89.
PHELPS, William 4.
PITTS, Sandra Jean 91, 92.
PLAGEMAN, Fred 34.
POAGUE, Alice 88.
PORTER, Patricia Elaine 83, 85.
POVALL, Robin 21, Sarah 21, 22.
POWELL, Caroline H. 63, 64, Dustin 36, John 64, Joyce 73, Steven 36, William 36.
PRICE, Daryen 83.
PURVIS, Charles 23, Curtis 29, 32, Gary Dewayne 32, Michael Lee 32, Pink 28, Polly 50, William Randolph 21.
RAY, James Harley 34.
REGISTER, Ernest 42, 43.
RELIFORD, Rebecca 44, 5.
RICKETSON, Eileen 35, 37, Eli 45, Ivy 60.

RICKS, Lewis 3, Patience 3, Sarah Ann 3.

RING, Helen 9.

ROBERTS, J. W. 12, 14, John W. 26, Lisa 79, 80, Ricky 14, Wilson 6.

ROGERS, Ida 56, Nancy Ann 53, 55, Thomas Morgan 55.

ROWE, Betty Elizabeth 90, 92, 93, Drew, Sr. 90, Ellender 38, James Edgar, Jr. 90, 91, James Edgar 90, 91, Jonathan Michaek 91, Laster 92, Mackie 72, Marsha Ann 90, 91, Melaine Diane 91, Teresa Elaine 90, Terry Lynn 90, 91.

ROWELL, Emory M. 13.

ROWLAND, Bernice 77, Caswell 64.

ROYALL, Henry 21, John 22, Joseph 20, 21, 22, Katherine 20, Sarah 20, 21, 22, William 20, 21, 22.

ROYALS, Annie Belle 35, 37, Bessie Mizell 33, 34, 37, 38, Betty Jo 35, 36, Christine 38, Clarence 35, 37, Clayton 35, 36, Clyde Wayne 37, Dewayne 38, Elton 35, 37, Joel William 35, 37, 38, Joelene 37, Johnny 38, Kay 38, Larry 38, Layton 36, Linda 38, Marsha 38, Patricia 38, Peggy 38, Rosa 38, Sarah Bell 36, Shirley 38, Willameana 37, Wilson 35, 37.

RUDOLPH, Katherine 97, Steve 97.

RUTHERFORD, Christopher James 87, Jack Dewitt 87, Jonathon Dewitt 87.

RYALS, Beadie Ann 33, Eliza Elizabeth 23, Elizabeth 22, Eliza 23, Emmer Percilla 33, Hattie 33, 42, 43, 44, Henry Melvin 33, Irene 32, 38, 39, 40, 41, James Calvin 23, 32, 33, 34, 35, 38, 42, 53, 66, John 22, Joseph 22, 23, Joshua C. 26, Lucy Ann 23, 24, Maria 23, Mary Ann 22, Mary Jane (Mollie) 33, 34, Matilda 23, Mollie Elizabeth 26, 27, 28, Nancy Elizabeth 33, 34, 35, Oren 23, 26, Penelope 22, Sabrey Carolina 11, 12, 33, 66, 67, 72, 82, 83, 86, 90, 95, Thomas 23, Tilitha 26, Wade Joshuaway 33, William G. 23, William Riley 22, 23, 24, 26, 32, 33, 52, William 22, 23, Winnifred 22.

SALMON, David Allen 75, Pete 73, 75, Steven 75.

SALVO, Georgette 75, 76.

SANDERSON, Dock 53.

SEARS, Bobby 28, Bryan 26, Cynthia Ann 29, Dorothy Lucille 28, 29, 30, Eunice (Una) 26, Floy 26, Geraldine 29, 32, Hamilton 26, Hansel Vernon 26, 27, 28, Hattie Elaine 29, Helen Jeanette 29, 31, 32, James Bryan, Jr. 29, James Bryan 28, 29, Mary 26, Mollie 27, 28, Nellie Francis 29, 30, 31, Rebecca 26, Ruby 27, 28, Solomon 26, 27, 28, Stanford 26, 28, 29, 30, 31, 32, Tobitha 26, 27, Virnnie 5, 9, Vollie 27, 28.

SELLERS, Amy 74, Mark 73, 74, Mary 74.

SELYE, Herbert 85.

SHATTO, Cynthia 14, 15, Ed 14, Michelle 14, Robert, Jr. 14, Robert 12, 14, 15, 16, Sharon 14, 16.

SIKES, Willie Neal 54.

SILAS, Mary Nell 35, 37, 38.

SITTON, Raymond Pierce 77, 79.

SLAVEN, Vickie Dianna 84, 85, Victor Lloyd 83, 84.

SMELLY, Elinor 2, Elizabeth 2, Giles 2.

SMITH, Benajah 51, E. B. 87, Lorrie 87, Myrtice 11, 83, Penny 87, Roger 55.

SNIPES, Arthur, Jr. 29, Eric Wayne 29, John Austin 29, Scott Bryan 29.

SOLES, Grace 90, Noley 74, Winnell 73, 74, 75.

SOLOMON, Ronnie 18.

SPELL, Dan Wade, Jr. 90, 91, Dan Wade, Sr. 91, Donna Lynn 32, Tara Danielle 91.

SPELLS, Jim 67.

SPIKES, Louise 87, Penny 6.

SPIVEY, Ella 67, Erica Daniell 81, Frank 5, James 46, Jan 89, Jimmy 89, Mark Andrew 89.

STEBBINS, Deacon Edward 47, Elizabeth 47.

STEEDLEY, Edna Robbin 37.

STEVENS, Fannie Alene 34, 35, Jimmy 27.

STEVERSON, Lois Marie 13.

STEWART, Andrew 33.

STONE, Maxie 6, Russell 6, 8, Vanna Joyce 8, Vonice 89.

STRICKLAND, Debbie 75, Rebecca 24, Theodore Hubert 34.

STUDSTILL, Viola 59.

SUMMERLIN, Allen 36, Cheryl 36, Janice 36, Joyce 36, Mack O'Neal 36, Sheila 36.

SUMNER, Ernest 88, Peggy 86, 88, 89.

SUTTON, Mary 36.

SWEAT, Brandi Leigh 16, Crystal Laneil 16, Kacey DaNean 16, Thomas W. 16, Wayne 12, 16.

SWEATS, J. C. 35, 37.

TANNER, Mary 46, Queen Victoria 26, 27, 28.

TAYLOR, Edwin Jerome 68, Elizabeth Cornelia 26, James Drury 68, Jeffery Jerome 68, Marie Alice 83, Mary Catherine 55, Robert 27, William 55.

TERRY, Nathaniel 22.

THOMAS, Amanda 17, 50, Bruce Patrick 31, 32, Jesse Helen 32, Marshall Patrick 32.

THOMPSON, Barbara June 77, 81, , Bonita 30, Emma Virginia 53, 54, Jesse 51, John 54, Lois 29, 30, Mitchell 18, Nora Jean 67, 68, Polly 59, Shannon Star 79, Temple Ann 30, Tommy Langston 78, 79.

TILLEY, Anelia Nerelle 84, Randy Michael 84.

TODD, John N. 67, Nellie Victoria Todd 11, 67, 68, 69.

TRANKS, Sharon Kay 69, 71.

TROYNECK, Pamela 90, 94, 95.

TUGGLE, Carrie 65.

TYNER, Mary Delree 34.

TYSON, Martha 46.

UNDERWOOD, Theophilus 2.

VARNADOE, Chung He (Varnadoe) 82, DeAnna Leigh 82, Denny Lee 82, Felix 82.

VICKERS, Kevin 92, 93, Mary Polly 26, Monica 97.

WALDRON, Annie 5, 6, 9, Delessie L. 6.

WALKER, Doris Geraldine 78. Ida Mae 34, Sudie Gertrude 53.

WALL, Frances Ellen 23.

WALLACE, Randell Dewayne 85, Randy Sameral 85.

WALLER, Lola Mae 42.

WATERS, An Jane 6.

WEEKS, William Hannibal 63.

WELLS, Antone Hutchison 34.

WHEELER, Rhonda 73, 74.

WHITE, Esther 58.

WHITEHURST, Sarah 24.

WILKINSON, John 20.

WILLIAMS, Charles 92, Christopher Lee 81, Dusti Marie 81, Mark Allen 91, 92, Samuel Allen 92.

WILLIAMSON, Charles 51, Nancy 51.

WILLIS, William Terrell 82.

WILSON, Joe E. 77, 78, 79, Judy 78, 79, Robert 47.

WISE, Henry 63.

WOLFANGER, Doris 67, 70.

WOOTEN, James Allen 43, Ty 43.

WORTHY, Bobby 74, Dennis 73, 74, James 73. Jennifer 74, Lewis Robert, Jr. 73, 74, Lewis Robert 73, 74, Rebecca 74, Sarah Mae 74.

# BIBLIOGRAPHY

1. SOME FAMILIES FROM THE HEART OF GEORGIA by Smallwood, Burch.
   Pages 128-136.

2. WILLS OF NASH COUNTY, N. C.. Abstracted by Dr. Stephen E. Bradley, Jr.
   Vol. I 1777-1848, p. 50, 255. Copyright 1992.

3. 1920 Atkinson County Census

4. 1860, 1870, 1880, 1900, 1910, 1920 Coffee County Census.

5. HISTORY OF COFFEE COUNTY, GEORGIA. by Warren P. Ward.
   Published by the Reprint Company Publishers, Spartanburg, S. C.

6. HISTORY OF DODGE COUNTY, GA. by Mrs. Wilton Philip Cobb.
   Published originally 1932, reprinted 1979 by the Reprint Company Publishers.
   p. 213-214, 221-225, 246-247.

7. KINFOLKS OF NASH COUNTY, N. C. by Joseph W. Watson.
   Published by Fisher-Harrison Corporation. Book 1, p. 5, 145, Book 3, p. 15,
   190, 331, 339, 403, 532.

8. SOME COLONIAL AND REVOLUTIONARY FAMILIES OF N. C.
   Vol. I, II, III, by Marilu Burch Smallwood. Published 1964.

9. HISTORY OF MONTGOMERY COUNTY, GA. by James E. Dorsey
   and John K. Derden. Copyright 1983. Published by the Reprint Company
   Publishers.

10. BURCH, HARRELL, AND ALLIED FAMILIES, Vol. I, II.
    by Marilu Burch Smallwood. Published by Storter Printing Co., Inc. Vol. I,
    p. 25-48, p. 95. Vol. II p. 434-452.

11. BURCH, HARRELL, AND ALLIED FAMILIES, Vol. III.
Written by Marilu Burch Smallwood. Compiled, edited, and indexed by Tad
Evans. p. 198, 381-395.

12. RELATED ROYAL FAMILIES, Vol. I & II, by Marilu Burch Smallwood.
Published 1974. p. 166-172, p. 213-214.

13. CONNER, RYALS, MCARTHUR FAMILY HISTORY by Mary Clyde McArthur
Published 1978. p. 217-220, p. 512-514.

14. JOINER-JOYNER by Ransey Joiner, Jr., Copyright 1974.
p. 1-8, Introduction, p. 46-50.

15. 1850 Pulaski County, Ga. Census

16. 1790 N. C. Census Index

17. 1800 N. C. Census Index

18. MONTGOMERY COUNTY MARRIAGES, Compiled by Debra Fennell.
May 1991.

19. THE VIRGINIA MAGAZINE OF HISTORY AND BIOGRAPHY.
Vol. XXXII for Year ending 12/31/1924
Vol. XXXIII for Year ending 12/31/1925

20. WHITES AMONG THE CHEROKEES, Written by the Participants.
Collected and edited by Mary B. Warren and Eve E. Weeks.
Copyright 1987 by Mary Bondurant Warren
Heritage Papers, Danielsville, Ga. 30633.

21. PIONEERS OF THE WIREGRASS, by Judge Folks Huxford.

# Andrew Cuomo's

## Time to Go...

# "He Was Never that Great!"

*Andrew Cuomo says America was 'never that great.' Get rid of him instead of America!*

Learn what Andrew Cuomo, the esteemed (by some) Governor of New York thinks of America by reading this book. It is the best thing you can do to understand why the Governor in our second largest state (tied with Florida by population) is so negative about our great country and its founding. This book not only gives Cuomo's perspective, and the perspective of his millennial followers, it is the best starter book for anybody wanting to refresh their knowledge or learn about America.

This book helps us all understand the founding and how its basic principles of government assure our freedom and liberty. Freedom and liberty may not be too important for The bold and brash and far left Andrew Cuomo, but for most Americans, there is nothing more important.

America's founders were smart, intelligent, and selfless men. The New York contingents from which Cuomo follows have been anti-American from when their representatives at the Constitutional Convention, John Lansing, and Robert Yates, chose not to sign the documents in support of the Constitution even though fellow statesman Alexander Hamilton chose to cast NY's vote as "aye."

When Pennsylvania's Benjamin Franklin said: "We must indeed all hang together or most assuredly, we shall all hang separately, he gave away the essence of the seriousness of the task facing America's founders. For as trite as some seem to portray the founding today, it was a serious undertaking by serious men who had been pushed around enough by King George. There is no reason from anybody to be ashamed of America today or its founding.

It is certainly unfortunate that our country is led by corrupt and greedy politicians, such as Andrew Cuomo and perhaps others of his ilk, who have taken control of many levels of governments in America. The good news is that most US citizens and others are hopping on the Train of Freedom to win back America from the forces of evil. Incompetent governors who hate conservatives in our society, such as Andrew Cuomo, son of Mario, are slow to learn but over time, Americans hope they too will get the real message. In the meantime, Americans pray that New Yorkers will never vote another Cuomo into office again.

This book is positioned as today's solution for *would-be* chumps to be better prepared to react to the overreach of praetorian politicians such as Andrew Cuomo and elite establishmentarians, who hope to set the country back three hundred years. With statements like 'America was never great,' it shows they would be happy to replace freedom with a hand-out-based government that controls the people and not vice-versa. Freedom loving people from across the world come here for freedom and opportunity. Those in this country who may say that America is not a great country should take a one-way trip to Russia or Mexico. Good riddance to Mr. Cuomo. Too bad he is trying to be reelected in NY only to stage his sorry self for a run for President. Americans must stop him.

This book is a quick way for you to learn about the real America and not the misimpressions of socialist progressive whackos and their millennial sycophants. . This book shows why the many blessings of our founding principles need not be replaced. Rather than get rid of America; a better option is to get rid of Cuomo, the current Governor of New York State.

Just because corrupt and powerful officials choose to ignore the rights and freedoms of American citizens does not mean we must endure their tyranny. The first step of course is to understand the founding and the most basic written precepts describing America and our rights as Americans. Reading this book about America's greatness is a must for every US citizen. I bet you will not be able to put this book down.

# BRIAN W. KELLY

Title   **Andrew Cuomo's Time to Go "He Was Never That Great."**

**Published by:**      LETS GO PUBLISH!
**Editor**             Brian P. Kelly
**Editor**             Brian P. Kelly
**Cover Design**       Brian W Kelly
**Web site**           www.letsgopublish.com

Library of Congress Copyright Information Pending
**Book Cover Design by Brian W. Kelly**

**ISBN Information:** The International Standard Book Number (ISBN) is a unique machine-readable identification number, which marks any book unmistakably.  The ISBN is the clear standard in the book industry. 159 countries and territories are officially ISBN members.  The Official ISBN for this book is also on the outside cover: _____  `_____

**978-1-947402-58-4**

The price for this work is:                                      **$9.95 USD**
10      9      8      7      6      5      4      3      2      1

Release Date:                                         September 2018